Roving Mad:

Odd Encounters

by

Malcolm Windsor

ISBN: 978-1-326-97056-7

Cover design by Scott Gaunt.

Preface

What makes an encounter memorable? Certain situations are unforgettable, and I believe they are to do with a little madness.

You might go to or have dealings with or suffer from actions by a mad country. Can a country go mad? Yes, I think it can. Some countries were insane, Hitler's Germany, Albania in the 1950s to 1990s, the Soviet Union until it broke up, Mao's China and Pol Pot's Cambodia. Had they been individuals, the actions they took would have led to them being declared insane or criminal or both. They would have been locked up. But that wasn't necessary: they locked themselves up.

You might meet someone who strikes you as strange –a common experience for most of us. Many individuals we meet in life may strike us as mad, eccentric, interesting, funny or scary, and we remember them. Maybe you yourself, or your travelling companion, do something mad or just silly.

But sometimes the encounter is so boring – like the nice people by the pool in Lanzarote who go on and on about cruises and how good the peas were on the Queen Mary – that you can't get rid of it either.
In this book there are encounters, in various parts of the world, that are strange and shocking, scary and funny. Though many of these are humorous, they also reveal something of the people, the epoch, the regime and the place.

Some names, dates and places have been changed.
A donation to mental health charities will be made from sales of this book

The Author

Malcolm Windsor is a scientist who experienced World War II as a child and, guided by his Aunty Gladys, learnt to hate Hitler at the early age of three. He travelled as much as possible when young and then as a scientist involved in national and international fisheries matters, always seeming to have jobs involving travel. Latterly the journeys were often to remote areas in various north Atlantic countries where there were salmon rivers and communities dependent upon them. He also underwent a long journey, which took five years by bicycle, but unfortunately always on the same route, cycling three nights a week to night school to study chemistry. Following this, he did a PhD and to California before returning to the UK.

He thinks that humour allows us to see things in perspective and so is a vital lubricant in human interactions. He hates bureaucracy but had to deal with lots of it in the British Civil Service, the European Commission and with many foreign governments. Many of these encounters with the public sector have surprising, mad or funny outcomes.

He lives in Edinburgh with his wife Sally.

Acknowledgements

I acknowledge the hundreds of people who supplied the fun, surprises, fear or intrigue described here. They have been good enough not to return the compliment and write about it from their viewpoint.

I thank my first wife, let's call her Margaret, who suffered from a great deal of mental illness and I am very proud of her for coming through it all. She came with me to Greece and Turkey, where events took an unfortunate turn. Her story here is only through my eyes but it is she who battled through it and, I am glad to say, eventually recovered well from what is one of the most dreadful maladies you can imagine.

My second wife, Sally, joined me notably in Albania, Chile, France and Russia. She was intrepid and marvellous company in sometimes strange situations and we could rejoice at the world in which these things happen and to laugh at it all – or most of it.

I thank my two wonderful daughters, Suzie and Sarah, both with a great sense of humour, who put up with my frequent absences and when I was at home suffered from nightly tests over dinner to name the world's capital cities. They could never remember the capital of Albania, who does? But now they do.

For my grandchildren too, Amber, Charlie, David, Jasmine, Saffron and Sean, so they may know, if they wish, a few of the odd things that happened to me.

Finally, sincere thanks to my editor Julie Fergusson and to David Morrison of PublishNation

Malcolm Windsor
Edinburgh
April 2017

Contents

Introduction: Why do we remember some things and not others?

William James once said, 'Whenever two people meet, there are really six people present. There is each man as he sees himself, each man as the other person sees him and each man as he really is.'

In the early 1980s I was walking along a street in Bath, far from Edinburgh, where I lived at the time. I glanced a tall, thin man coming towards me with quite a silly walk, more of a lope. He passed me but then swung on his heel and grabbed my shoulder hard, so I spun around too. We were eyeball to eyeball. 'Didn't you used to be Malcolm Windsor?' he said. There was an accusatory tone in his voice. My mind raced. Should I admit it? Maybe he wanted to kill me… I thought it best to come clean. 'Yes, I used to be.'

He stared at my face intently, as if he thought I was lying. Then he seemed reassured. I started to ask, 'Do we know each oth…?' but he interrupted. 'Do you know you've got a moustache?' he barked. Well, in that time many people had a moustache (and flared trousers and orange wallpaper too). I thought I'd better admit to the moustache too as I sensed that otherwise he might try to rip it off and claim that I was an imposter.

He let go of me and loped off. I never found out who he was and, though my moustache is long gone, I still remember it (the encounter, not the moustache).

There were rather a lot of mad people, most also with moustaches, running whole countries in the last century: in Hitler's Germany, Stalin's Russia, Mao's China and Hoxha's Albania. The madness hasn't stopped today, it has just moved elsewhere. It is still endemic in North Korea and of course in the Islamic caliphate called ISIS. The UN should open a lunatic asylum for countries and call it UNLAS. North Korea has locked itself up, but ISIS seems set on spreading its lunacy to the rest of us. It is not too surprising that in each country there are a small minority of mad people with weird, often cruel, ideas. It is less easy to understand how they manage to rise through national organisations to attain positions of power. And it is even more perplexing that, somehow, they are considered so charismatic and persuasive that they convince millions of others to do as they say – even if their edicts are clearly cruel, mad and abhorrent.

We humans have repeatedly shown a willingness to project God-like powers and wisdom onto damaged and irrational people, just take the four above. But why? Is it a genetic fault in our make-up?

4

There are other countries I have never been to that show signs of being mad. Yemen, for example, seems to be driving itself and its neighbours mad and, to pick one at random, in Guinea-Bissau no President has ever served his term and the poor chap in power in 2003 was arrested and imprisoned for something politically normal elsewhere – 'failing to solve the problems'. In Venezuela, which has one of the biggest oil reserves on earth, the regime has managed to create an economy where you queue up for hours to buy a toilet roll. God knows if the People's Republic of the Congo is sane but I don't want to go and find out. Even in the US, many politicians seem to believe that the way to stop people with guns going on killing rampages is to give everyone else a gun as well.

The chances of having a memorable encounter are high if you go to a country that has gone mad and locked itself up. Life becomes distorted under such maniacal regimes. Many of the encounters I describe here were in countries living under communism, one of those ideas that looked good on paper, especially to social scientists or economists. President Ronald Reagan was once stuck in a room with a group of political economists who were banging on about how to run something or other owned by the federal government. They had done a theoretical study and were trying to persuade him to adopt it. He had been governor of California and had run something similar there, so he came up with an alternative proposal, which he said he knew from personal experience worked in practice. This stopped them in their tracks. After a pause, the senior economist came back to Reagan. 'Mr President, from what you say your idea might work in practice. But what concerns us is… does it work in theory?'

The Soviet Union, then the biggest country in the world, was locked into a massive social experiment based on theories by Marx, Lenin, Engels and Trotsky. It was designed to halt capitalism and create a society where everyone was equal and equally remunerated. Everything was owned and managed by the state, so no need for private profit. The workers' interests would always be put first. They called it the dictatorship of the proletariat. The big mistake was that it contravened most aspects of human nature: the urge to compete, get on in life, be independent, to prosper, to have things of your own, to have the right to speak freely and to think for yourself. None of these were encouraged or even allowed.

The USSR doggedly kept at the experiment even when almost everyone living there knew it had failed. By the end there were practically no communists left, though a few today still long for the good old days under Stalin. The fact that the government was based on fear added a certain frisson, as you knew everyone you met had to be careful not to speak their mind. They were living in a society which was failing them but they dared not say so. Leaving the country after a visit, there was a sadness, as if saying goodbye to a friend in prison. For it was a prison: they could not leave without permission hard to come by.

A few got out on temporary permits, like those I met who were chosen to represent the USSR in international fisheries negotiations. When I received the first Soviet delegation in Edinburgh for salmon fishery negotiations in 1985 the five of them brought all their own food for the week. Jars of pickled cucumber, logs of fatty black sausage, screw-top bottles of vodka and even their bread for the week. They sat on the carpeted floor in the Sheraton hotel, luxuriating in their vests eating and drinking until they passed out. I wondered why they didn't take the chance to enjoy the western food – a steak maybe, fresh vegetables, wine. It would be a nice change from gristly sausage and cucumber, so I thought. But that wasn't the name of the game. The chance to come to a meeting in the west meant the chance to get hard currency.

While they were abroad they received a daily allowance from the government. If they lived on the black sausages and pickles, they would have hard currency they could take home. Their own money was essentially worthless; only exchangeable for Soviet goods, which were shoddy. There were shops in the USSR selling Scotch whisky, Cadbury's chocolates and Sony TVs but they wouldn't accept roubles, only foreign money. I tried to imagine what it would be like if all the shops in Edinburgh sold terrible goods and terrible food, with one shop that sold the good stuff I wanted but wouldn't take my money. What kind of workers' paradise was that?

When I travelled to Russia myself for the first time I was shocked: things were ramshackle, worn out and ugly. But not everything was like that – their rockets and atom bombs still worked. The Russians were intensely friendly and hungry for contact with the outside world. There was a special warmth when you sat around a table with them, and not just due to the massive amounts of vodka always available. This distorted society often threw up situations that could not be imagined elsewhere. Even though the disastrous social experiment has ended, the new Russia can be odd too: in their recovering society anything goes, even plucking aeroplanes out of the sky for your personal use – if you have some money.

6

Bristol: The Anderson shelter (1941)

A terrible example of a country going mad is, of course, when Hitler took over Germany. As a three year old I knew nothing of countries or politics, but what I did see, which was exciting, was a lorry piled high with strange, wavy sheets of iron, driving behind the back-garden fences of our row of houses. At each house the men threw eight pieces of corrugated iron into the garden, six of which were curved at one end. They flattened the cabbages, which was good and intensely interesting too: what were they for? Considering the good news about the cabbage destruction I didn't ask my mother.

The next day, more men came and dug a deep hole in our garden, putting the earth in a big pile on the side which finished off the remaining cabbages and a few stringy broccolis. This was even more exciting. Then a third team of men came and stuck the six curved pieces in the ground so the ends formed a rounded roof and then they bolted them together. The flat pieces formed the ends, and they fitted a metal door, too. It only took them twenty minutes and then they covered the whole lot with the excavated earth and put the turf back on top. Now it was just a new hump in the garden adorned with dead cabbage.

Then a lorry dropped wooden bunks over the back fence which fitted exactly inside, making it the perfect den. I didn't know that any of this was because of Hitler. I just loved it and wanted to go and stay in it there and then. I didn't have a Dad – they said he was away in the war – but my mother, Nancy, came out and looked at it and she didn't seem to like it as much as I did. She peered into the gloom, looked at the earthen floor and the wooden bunks and shuddered. She was twenty-one years old.

A few weeks later the sirens sounded and we hurriedly put on warm clothes, went downstairs and out into the garden. The shelter didn't look so nice at night: dark, dank and cold, and already full of spiders, who loved it more than I did. Mum and I clung together on one bunk bed until the all-clear siren sounded. The bombers always came at night. Aunty Gladys, who lived alone next door but one and only ever seen in a floral wrap-around apron, usually joined us in the shelter. Sometimes I craned my head out of the door and saw the aircraft above us, dropping their bombs with great flashes of light – thankfully not near us most of the time. 'Hitler! They Germans,' Gladys would shout, half at me and half at them.

I don't remember being scared but I could not understand why 'Hitler', whoever he was, wanted to kill me. What had I done to him?

7

As I discovered much later, Gladys had good reason for her hatred: her fiancé had been killed in World War I and she had never married. There was a terrible shortage of men after that war.

Gladys was charged with looking after me if Mother went out. She was constantly convinced that the Germans were about to drop poison gas on St George, the suburb of Bristol where we lived. I suppose she didn't want to be held responsible for any injury to me resulting from a sudden decision by Hitler to drop poison gas on Hillside Road and, consequently, she only let me go out to play with the other boys if I wore my gas mask, with its Mickey Mouse logo. I much resented being the only boy in Hillside Road, or more likely in the West of England, or even in the whole galaxy, obliged to play cricket against the lamp post in a Mickey Mouse gasmask but it was better than staying indoors with Gladys.

She was nervous of my every move and scanned the skies like a homemade early warning system for an aircraft that might have missed the RAF's attention. The local lads teased me unmercifully about this and I got so hot and sticky in the wretched thing that I sneaked it off when the coast was clear. But Gladys checked on me, coming out to the front gate and shouting, 'Get your gas mask on my boy, they Germans are about!' Despite my embarrassment, I took it, in an unquestioning way, that Aunty Gladys knew more about Hitler's intentions for Hillside Road than anyone else did.

Later in my boyhood I discovered that Gladys worked for the war effort at what was quaintly called the 'the corset factory' in Redfield, two miles in towards Bristol. Then it dawned on me that those engaged in manufacturing ladies' corsets, even at the highest command levels – which Gladys was not – were not in the best position to discover Hitler's bombing strategy for the West of England. I realised she had no access to such information and I need not have worn the gas mask at all.

My mother talked about 'Dad' but I had no idea what a Dad was. A few boys seemed to have one but most men were away. She told me that Dad was in the Dutch East Indies and then she told me later that he had moved to India. Now and again, a parcel arrived with exotic stamps showing ladies with three pairs of arms, each with gold bangles. It puzzled me that Indian ladies had more arms than Mum and Aunt Gladys. In the parcels there was often a toy for me and something for Mum, once the parcel had a painted segmented snake for me. I pulled it around the floor and up the stairs and it would wriggle with life. In the same package was a tin for Mum, Indian canned butter. It had a faintly rancid flavour, a soft semi-melted texture and a yellow colour. The product evidently did not survive the ending of hostilities.

The years until primary school passed without a father, and by 1943, Mother and I were buddies, she with no husband, I with no father. Though he existed I had no recollection of him whatsoever, so he was linked in my mind with images of India, garish wooden toys and tins of butter. My mother must have almost forgotten him too after so many years. Maybe she forgot his face, as you do if you have not seen someone for years. So many hopes and fantasies must have been embedded in his homecoming.

I toddled off to Air Balloon Hill Primary Mixed School. For the first few weeks, Mother took me, but after that she said I should walk down the road myself, only 800 yards. I wasn't too keen but she said that I was a big boy now, she would take me to our front garden gate and I would be fine. On my first big boy day I walked quickly backwards down the road, waving at Mum constantly, snivelling to myself, clutching my Mickey Mouse gas mask and willing her to keep eye contact, to stay at the front garden gate and watch me until I was out of sight. It worked well for the first fifty yards but I forgot the telegraph pole on that bit of pavement. I walked into it backwards, still waving madly, smacked my head hard against it and crumpled half-conscious onto the pavement.

The teachers were all elderly ladies. All the male teachers were away at war or in essential jobs connected with the war effort, as were the young female teachers. Our teachers had been dragged out of retirement and, apart from one or two, seemed to resent it. They all wore severe tweed suits. Miss Johnson wore only two suits, identical in every respect except one was green and the other red. I fancied she was in a worse mood when she wore the green. In such a female environment the boys became more macho and on my first day at school I was impressed to see a competition in the boy's toilets as to who could pee the highest up the wall. It wasn't safe in there but it was getting safer outside as the bombing stopped.

Our Anderson shelter was falling into disuse but we boys used it every day as a marvellous den. There was talk between Mum and Gladys of the war ending. That apparently meant my Dad would come home from India. What would it be like? I didn't realise that it would change everything – and not in a good way.

Clevedon: Isolation hospital (1945)

The Dad from India who was only there because of the mad Hitler had still not appeared as I approached seven in 1945 and fell ill with Scarlet fever. It was common. This meant going into hospital because antibiotics had not come into use and there was no cure. I was diagnosed by the elderly GP for half a crown and sent to hospital in an ambulance, which was a real playground asset. When the boys bragged in the playground, 'My brother's bigger than your brother,' 'My Dad's stronger than your Dad,' I always made a surprise attack: 'I've been in an ambulance and you haven't.' The isolation hospital was near Clevedon, a small town near Bristol with a pebble beach on the Severn Estuary.

All the boys there had Scarlet Fever and we were in one long ward, maybe thirty of us. I didn't feel too ill, but the elderly matron told me I was forbidden to get out of bed. None of us were allowed up, in fact. The staff believed in complete bed rest with plenty of fresh air, so the windows were wide open night and day and great gusts of freezing air swept off the pebble beach through the ward. One by one during the day each boy was taken to a central table where there were several enamel bowls and jugs. Our thick woolly pyjamas were expertly removed and we were washed down with flannels and carbolic soap in front of the others. Matron, who stood no nonsense, had obviously been trained at a secret camp in the Clevedon dunes by the West of England SS. When she flannelled you down and briskly towelled you dry there was a certain amount of body contact but no sensation of being in contact with female flesh. She was evidently a client of Aunty Gladys's, solidly corseted.

After our tea of bread and margarine sandwiches with condensed milk, Matron would disappear and we were left unsupervised. A few Bravehearts jumped out of bed and raced around the room pulling off pyjamas and sheets and stealing sweets. I was not brave enough to do that, one of the youngest there. But we made paper aeroplanes under the sheets and then pulled them out when there were no nurses and tried to fly them into the enamel bowls on the long central table. If you were lucky the next victim selected for washing found his water full of soggy paper. I seemed to be in the isolation hospital forever. Then one day my mother arrived and announced that my father was coming home. She was excited but it meant little to me since I had no memory of him. He had gone away to the war in the Far East when I was three. She said

10

that Matron told her I could come home in five days. I returned to the paper aeroplanes.

Then, one day, Matron came up to me with more than usual urgency. 'Malcolm Windsor, you are going home and your father is in my office waiting to take you.' Father? Office? I did not know what each word meant. She helped me dress; I hadn't worn clothes for three or four weeks and they felt heavy. She led me from the ward through a side door that I had not noticed before. A man stood there in army uniform, his cap tucked into the epaulette on his shoulder and with a badge that read REME. He looked anxious; thin but deeply tanned compared to most men around. 'This is your father,' said Matron. He leant down and picked me up. I resisted.

Who was this strange man in a strange uniform? Why was my mother not here? Matron chided me: 'This is your father, you've got to give him a big welcome home from India, from the war.' But I did not know this strange man and I did not want to welcome him home from the war. I wanted him to go back to the war and I certainly did not want him to pick me up. Matron forced me out of the front door but I was reluctant to leave and would have happily climbed back into bed in the Scarlet Fever ward if she had let me. I trudged disconsolately alongside the man, feeling unsure and upset that my mother hadn't come. How could I be sure this was my father?

We took a country bus back into town and then the city bus to Hillside Road. By the time, we got home I was furious with Mother. I felt betrayed that she should send this stranger to collect me. For all my life, so far, it had been just her and me, but now we were a threesome and I realised with a dull disappointment that life had changed – and not for the better. Where I had been the centre of her attention for those war years, now there was a much bigger boy around. She reacted to him differently than to me. Of course, I did not know the word flirtatious but that was what I was seeing in her, a side I had never seen and I didn't much care for it. I was side-lined now.

In retrospect, how could I blame her after those long years on her own? It must have been a second honeymoon. But at the time, at the age of six or seven, I did blame her. I was severely disgruntled. Worst of all, I was kicked out of her bed. Mum and I had slept side by side during the whole war. I did not much like the peace and hoped that soon there might be another war.

11

Bristol: Science and soluble aspirin, the wrong result (1954)

At sixteen I began my first job, at Ferris's a Manufacturer of Pharmaceutical Products and Surgical Appliances, in a rundown part of Bristol. This was to be the start of my scientific career. At eight o'clock on Monday morning I made my way there, but I couldn't find the staff entrance. The place was made up of four seedy-looking Georgian houses joined together, the front doors I tried didn't open. I followed a group of girls who were chattering and walking fast to get in on time. They veered around to the back and entered by a grubby door ringed with medical rubbish in bins: reels of gauze, laboratory glassware, cracked acid flasks and empty jars of gelatine and detergent.

I climbed a wooden staircase with loose handrails and found a door with a top half of frosted glass. On the glass was etched the word LABORATORY. This was it. I knocked on the door; there was no answer so I entered. It was a narrow room, dingy and with a smell of gas. At the far end was a tiny office, the top half of the wall clear glass, and another door on which was etched the word CHEMIST. This chemist was the scientist I had come to work for in this small and soon-to-be extinct firm called Ferris's.

The chemist's name was Mr Green and he had interviewed me the week before. He seemed short-tempered to me, and asked me tricky questions: 'How would you prepare chlorine gas in ten minutes?' The ten-minute requirement threw me. He then asked, 'What is the chemical formula for aspirin and soluble aspirin?' I didn't know. I was sure I had done badly in the interview and there were many applicants who could prepare chlorine in even two minutes and rattle off the chemical formulas for aspirin, Dettol and indigestion tablets.

So I was surprised to receive his letter offering me the job, to start on £2.17.6 per week. What was more, I was worried that in the intervening days I had forgotten to put myself straight on these questions. What if my first job was to produce chlorine gas by ten past eight? Without the O Level textbook I didn't think I could do it in ten days. In any case I had not the faintest idea what Mr Green did with the chlorine gas. But Mr Green was, on this first day of my scientific career, already in his office and had not spotted me in the laboratory. I soon saw why. He was engaged in close conversation with a young lady of about twenty. They were both in a good humour and I was relieved to see this, hoping it might mean chlorine gas production was not urgently required.

12

Because of the glass partition I did not hear their conversation but when he did catch sight of me crossing the laboratory his face took on a much more serious appearance. He was young, no more than thirty, and wore a largish black moustache and a white laboratory coat. He and the young lady saw me clearly but they finished off whatever they were discussing. I knocked at the door and Mr Green looked out through the glass as if I were a disagreeable schoolboy, which I was. In 1954, teenagers dressed like old men – there were no teenage clothes – so I might not have appeared shocking, but looking back I think it must have dawned on him that from now on he had this awkward youth hanging around, gawping through the glass partition during these early morning intimacies with Gill. That was her name and she was the laboratory assistant. Gill was a few years or so older than me, lively and warm. Although she smelt of disinfectant I liked her a lot more than Mr Green. Gill squeezed out of the narrow office, past a one-bar electric fire and past Mr Green.

With the bare minimum of formalities and no welcoming words of any kind, he took me through the procedures involved in starting work at Ferris's. There was a form to sign to absolve Ferris's of any blame should I blow myself up in their laboratory. Mr Green then walked out of the laboratory, instructing Gill to look after me. I was pleased and delighted by this because she was a friendly and warm person, at least towards Mr Green, and I was desperately lacking in confidence and still worried about the possible need for speedy manufacture of chlorine gas. Although I learnt chemistry at school and had done well in the exams, and was excited about working in a chemistry laboratory, I had never done any chemistry in real life.

Gill turned out to be as friendly as she seemed and we both spent long periods simply washing up burettes, pipettes and other laboratory glassware. There were moments of intimacy for me too: we sat by the electric fire in Mr Green's office if he was out, which he was most of the time. When he came back, he didn't show any irritation that I was huddled by the electric fire if Gill was there too. I would not have dared to do it alone, no matter how cold the laboratory was.

The company made medicines and surgical goods; it was also a small supplier of laboratory glassware and equipment to schools. Though no one ever explained it, our job was to check that the drugs and chemicals being turned out and sold were what they were supposed to be and they were at the right concentration. Much of the output was in the form of tablets and pills, mostly aspirin, and my first job was to measure the rate of dissolution of the day's batch of aspirin. I took

13

twelve tablets at random, placed them in a small metal basket and agitated the basket in a water bath held at a fixed temperature until the last aspirin dissolved. The time taken for this series of events to occur was recorded with a stopwatch. I was to write down the number of seconds this took and place the form in Mr Green's basket in his warm office.

I imagined that there was a certain time of dissolution, which, if exceeded, caused Mr Green to reject the batch. If so, he didn't mention it. On the third day I placed in his basket a report on a batch of aspirin that took 105 seconds to dissolve rather than the usual forty seconds or so. Mr Green did not accept my scientific result. He told me that it must be wrong, they were always less than fifty seconds. I was in the wrong, not the aspirin.

After that happened three times and I was castigated for getting it wrong I consulted Gill who told me that, whatever the actual result, I should adjust the time to be within his limits. It is only a short step from there to not bothering to carry out the test at all. It was against all the principles of scientific rigour we learnt at school but I grudgingly did as I was told, fearing Mr Green's short temper. It seemed to be the company policy. But I often wondered if there were customers walking around with insoluble Ferris's aspirin stuck in their bloodstreams. Clearly Mr Green did not want to be troubled by any scientific truths. It was not a good start.

Mr Green was mostly moody and offhand with me. He made no attempt to train me but left it to Gill. The firm was strangely run and there was a muted panic in the air for its future. One man, oddly smart for a surgical appliance operative and wearing an unusually clean white coat and gleaming black shoes, came into the laboratory every day at the same time. At first I couldn't work out what he was doing, though small sums of money were changing hands. The surgical appliance department employed him; in fact, he was the manager. But he spent each day on his rounds of the business taking bets, a pharmaceutical bookmaker. He was exceedingly cheerful and whistled a lot. He clearly enjoyed the daily chance to banter with the staff on his way around the premises, making detailed notes in a little note book kept in the top pocket of his white coat. I liked him because he raised morale, always making people laugh, but he never invited me to place a bet and I never asked. Not that I knew what they were betting on.

The employees were happy enough; indeed, after the bleakness of grammar school, Ferris's struck me as a happy sort of place. On my journeys down the back stairs at lunchtime each day, many of the young male and female factory workers would be sitting on the bare wooden stairs, one couple at each landing, talking and giggling together. If I was a little late at lunchtime things would have got heavy and they were half lying across the steps, fondling each other, oblivious to my diurnal migration up and down the back stairs. Those who did notice me must have assumed I was one of the 'staff', the lucky ones. With an electric fire and Gill in the laboratory I suppose I was. This lunchtime passion on the back stairs made me feel left out.

But Gill was friendly and the days spent in the same small room with the occasional physical contact as we moved between the laboratory benches or squeezed into the office in front of the electric fire gave me a sense of participation in what seemed, judging from the activities on the back staircase, to be one of the functions of the old firm. Mr Green was there less and less as my first few weeks passed by, only an hour or so in the mornings and half an hour last thing in the afternoon.

One day he asked me to do a titration. A titration involves adding a certain concentration of acid, for example, to a product that is alkaline, to ascertain the exact amount of acidity required to neutralise the alkalinity and thus tell how strongly alkaline the product is. To do the titration, as I learned at school, you added an indicator, usually a dye that changed colour at the stage when neutrality was reached. Mr Green seemed to think I should know exactly what to do although I hadn't done it outside the school lab. When I asked what indicator I should use he looked exasperated and pointed at a small table covered with dozens of small bottles and tubes. 'That one, boy, that one,' he spat irritably and turned back to the electric fire. With fear in my heart and not thinking straight from the panic of doing my first unsupervised titration, I wondered which bottle or tube on the small table he had pointed to. Gill, my protector, was away collecting samples of the day's disinfectant production so I could not turn to her.

In desperation, after an agony of indecision, I took the substance that was the closest to the target of his angry finger. It was gooey and in a tube but it was the one at which he had pointed, so I squeezed a little of it into the flask and started the titration. I added the acid solution slowly, waiting for the magic moment when the contents of the small laboratory flask changed colour and I duly recorded the amount of acid used. But I practically filled the flask and no change was to be seen in the murky contents. I got a flask twice the size, tipped the contents of my flask into the bigger one and continued the titration. Still no change.

I got a giant flask from the cupboard to continue but used so much of the acid that I stopped to make up more. At this point Mr Green must have seen me lurking with a giant litre flask when a tiny one was always sufficient. 'What on earth are you doing?' he shouted. I mumbled something incoherent into my giant flask and empty burette. 'What's that stuff in it?' At least I could answer that and I pointed to the tube from which I had taken my 'indicator'. His face reddened and he became temporarily speechless before exploding: 'You fool, you idiot! That is the stopcock grease for lubricating the burette!' He turned away in a fury while I swilled the contents of my giant flask down the sink as Gill came back in.

This was the big wide world that the geography teacher had talked about and I didn't seem to be much of a success in it. Mr Green's attitude, particularly regarding the testing of the aspirin, was acutely shocking to me. Why have a laboratory at all if you made up the results? It was scientific madness. I didn't like falsifying the solubility of the aspirin – it was demoralising for a budding scientist, even if so far a completely incompetent one. I handed in my notice to Mr Green. 'I'm not surprised,' he said wearily. 'You've been nothing but trouble!'

Keynsham: The chocolate laboratory and Uncle Reg (1954)

My next job was in the laboratory of Fry's chocolate factory, owned by Cadbury. Fry's, Cadbury and Rowntree's dominated the industry and all were Quakers. I was surprised that the Quakers concentrated on making chocolates, as it seemed a frivolous business for a sternly religious sect. But they were originally apothecaries who first sold cocoa as a medicinal product that was also a good alternative to alcohol, which they were dead against. Chocolate was an 'innocent trade'. The laboratory at the chocolate firm was much larger than Ferris's, with a staff of thirty, and the conditions were superior – warm, light and airy. Being Quakers they cared more: they paid most of my evening class fees and half of the cost of my books.

The factory was surrounded by meadows and was in a large loop of the River Avon in Somerset. The fields and woods were easily seen from the windows, and on hot summer days I looked longingly out from the gassy and hot air of the laboratory. I keenly felt a loss of liberty; I was now be expected to work for fifty weeks out of the fifty-two in the year, and this filled me with gloom. It seemed inhuman; at least at school there were the holidays. At sixteen I did not feel I had the freedom of the great wide world that had been promised me. My father

16

was keen on me leaving school at sixteen rather than staying on into the sixth form, and now I was trapped. He was convinced it was best to leave school, get a job and study at night school. Paradoxically, he was keen on education and often purchased educational books.

Uncle Reg, one of his ten older brothers, lived next door but one to us. Reg was a kindly man and now and then gave me a shilling, but he always seemed distracted, thinking of something else. He had had a terrible time at Arnhem in the war and wore a nervous air. He suffered a migraine every single weekend, which came on exactly when he got home from work on Friday night and lasted until Monday morning. His weekends were spent on the settee with a towel over his head. But he was keen on knowledge. I remember one set of books called The Complete Self Educator, which he bought jointly with my father. It was expensive and came in twenty chocolate brown gold embossed volumes, so they shared it. When it arrived I was excited: if I read it all and remembered it all I would be completely educated.... forever. What put me off was that I didn't see Reg becoming any more knowledgeable. In fact, Reg was more and more depressed after he took delivery.

The plan was that he had possession of the first ten volumes for the first three months and we had the second ten. Dad was a carpenter so he installed a heavy-duty shelf for ours, but we thought it wasn't wise to become Completely Self Educated by starting halfway through. We couldn't start with Volume 11. That might lead to you being Half Completely Self-Educated or Educated The Wrong Way Round. We decided to wait for Reg to finish his ten volumes first. Trouble was that his wife Edna was not at all happy with the purchase; she resented the expenditure and made it clear she would have very much preferred something else that they didn't have, like a fridge. She thought that Reg was as Completely Educated as was necessary for him to drive his electric truck at the chocolate factory. In any case, there was no room for it as Edna's ceramic ducks, which she was fond of, were strung up the wall.

She made Reg create a giant new bookshelf over the sofa in the sitting room. Reg had made a brave stand against Germany but he was not good at carpentry. That may have been partly what depressed him as from what I saw he could never get the shelf straight: the wall was peppered with Rawlplugs, as if Reg had used it for target practice. There was a real risk of Volume 1 or Volume 10 – or all of them – sliding off and braining Reg or Edna, or Gladys, who was a frequent visitor, or possibly all three. There was the possibility that ten people

17

might have been concussed simultaneously, as the three-piece suite was in that vulnerable zone under the shelf. A sudden blow to Gladys's head from Volume 1 might have increased her intelligence more swiftly than reading it. Reg made a start on his new education but his depression worsened and he was even off sick for three weeks. Dad and I didn't read it after seeing the effect on Uncle Reg.

Remaining incompletely self-educated, I was still sixteen and now in the science of confectionery. It was big business as the Brits had the sweetest teeth in the world. It wasn't just cocoa that the Quakers made anymore, it was chocolate bars. In the laboratory we had two tasks: first, to test the composition and safety of deliveries of all the ingredients that arrived from all over the world; second, to come up with new ideas for chocolate bars and try them out. The first task was boring but the second one was fun. We started with what was in store or we could get hold of. The factory always kept chocolate, egg albumen, milk powder, wafers, toffee, brazil nuts, peanuts, cashew nuts, raisins, currants, gelatine, attar of roses (for Turkish Delight), fragrances and essences of lemon and orange in store. But how to put these together in new ways? Fry's made well-known products, such as their Turkish Delight, Five Boys chocolate bar and the Crunchie.

To make a Crunchie bar you made a hot sugar syrup in a big tray and then bubbled air through it as it was setting. Then you sliced it up and covered it in milk chocolate. It was a great product, but the big problem was cutting it into slices. If you cut it with knives it shattered and you produced millions of pieces of crunch – impossible to make into a bar. This was eventually solved by cutting it with a giant lattice of thin, electrically heated wires. These sliced through it and each bar was then enrobed with chocolate. When I was there, we were developing a new bar: the Picnic bar. We tried all sorts of combinations but they were either too sweet or too hard or looked odd or fell to bits or couldn't be mass-produced. It wouldn't work to have hundreds of variations of the Picnic bar, all different shapes and compositions, emerging from the Fry's factory. I thought it would be nice, like ugly vegetables, but they would all have to have a different price. Not on.

The secret ingredient, which we did not stock but which many of us ate at home for breakfast, was Rice Krispies. That did the trick; we mixed them with the peanuts to coat the outside with a nice knobbly structure that the chocolate eagerly soaked up. And so the Picnic bar was born, and it is still going. My part in the development of the Picnic bar may have given the public more pleasure than anything else I have ever done but created a lot of fat people too. I didn't think of it at the

18

time as no one was obese then, even those who worked in the chocolate factory. I brought an experimental Picnic bar home for Uncle Reg and it cheered him up, and his depression lifted. But Edna was right – Reg was as up to speed as he needed to be education-wise, he just needed chocolate. The last time I saw Volume 1 it was propping up the bedside table in Reg and Edna's bedroom. Reg had made the table but one leg was shorter than the other three by just the thickness of Volume 1.

I cycled to night school three times a week in what always seemed to be driving rain. There I studied chemistry from 6:15 p.m. to 9:15 p.m. Most of my fellow students gave up but I was stubborn and pedalled on, until five years later – after innumerable punctures and with strong calves – I passed the exams to gain a Higher National Certificate in Chemistry. Phew! It was time to explore the world outside of soluble aspirin and Picnic bars.

Dingle, Ireland: Mrs O'Brady's price list (1957)

A new girl, Margaret, joined the Fry's laboratory and we had fun together in the darkroom where we measured the concentration of sucrose using polarised light. She and I decided to join up and take a holiday travelling around Ireland by local bus. We got to the far south-west, reaching a village called Dingle. It was just as an Irish village should be. Lots of small shops belonging to drapers, grocers or ironmongers, and nearly all of them with a barrel of Guinness on the counter. We liked it very much and decided to stay a week. I asked in the ironmongers about accommodation in the little town. 'Mrs O'Leary down there on the right lets out rooms. Try her,' I was told.

We walked up the road to Mrs O'Leary but she had nothing free. She pointed up the street and said to try Mrs O'Brady, who let out a caravan in her yard. The house was big with six stone steps up to the front door. I spotted the battered caravan in the garden. I knocked and the door opened to a thin woman, hair in a scarf, wearing a flowered apron. She folded her arms, looked down at us with disdain and said nothing. 'Good morning,' I stuttered. 'We're looking for accommodation and Mrs O' Leary said you have a caravan to rent out.' Her look of disdain did not alter as she studied us suspiciously. She looked up and down the street. 'Is it married you are?' A negative answer would have us back down the stone steps fast. 'Yes, we are,' I blurted out. She looked as if she knew I was lying and there was another silence. She seemed to come to a difficult decision against her better judgement. She unfolded her arms. 'It's a pound a night or eight pounds a week,' she said.

Now it was my turn for indecision. I hadn't ever come across of this form of pricing, where there was a penalty for staying longer. Perhaps there were there nine or ten nights in a Dingle week? Was she poor at arithmetic? 'That's fine, Mrs O'Brady. I'm not sure how long we'll be here, so we will pay by the day.' We stayed a week and paid seven pounds.

The Balkans: Left behind the Iron Curtain (1960)

It was time to explore the world and I decided to see the ancient world of Greece. Margaret said she wanted to come with me so I purchased two single tickets to Athens from London by rail. They were cheap, £11 each, the journey organised by the German Student Travel Service. When the tickets arrived I saw that we left Victoria at 8 a.m. on a Monday morning and didn't get to Athens until night-time on Thursday. The day before the train left, Margaret and I set off, hitchhiked to London and stayed the night with a friend, John Fortune, who was doing well in the satire business. The next morning, we boarded the train in Victoria station bound for Athens. There were no charter flights in those days and I hadn't flown in my life so the idea of taking four days to reach Athens did not seem strange.

After crossing to the Hook of Holland, the train arrived in Munich the same night and we took a cheap hotel. Our train to Greece did not leave until the next evening so we stocked up for the long journey through southern Germany, Austria, communist Yugoslavia and over the border to Greece. There were no restaurant facilities on the train and they said that under communism it was difficult to buy food in Yugoslavia so we bought tins of fish and meat, tomatoes, lots of bread and orange squash. The other passengers were all young German students who, stereotypically, ate prodigious amounts of black sausage and bread and drank Munich beer day and night. We crossed into Austria and were entranced by the scenery. The train must have been travelling slowly to take so long to get to Athens, but it meandered like a lazy snake through the Austrian mountains as it headed towards the border. The Germans finally stopped eating and drinking that night and we found separate sleeping niches, like pigeons in a loft at nightfall. One heavy young German slept on the net luggage rack above us and I was anxious that Margaret and I might be flattened by a direct hit from a beer belly during the night. But the train weaved to and fro and when we awoke we were at the border.

I was apprehensive. Communism was a frightening word in those days and the Iron Curtain was a reality. Yugoslavia was the most liberal Communist regime but, even so, the controls were rigid and time-consuming. The train sat for hours in the August morning haze but then, without any warning, lurched forward across the Iron Curtain and into Yugoslavia. We saw a big change; it looked much poorer than Germany and Austria. There were more people in the fields and there were no cars or trucks, just farmers on horses and carts. The speed of the train was cut to fifteen or twenty miles per hour and when it stopped it was for a long time. Each time it restarted it was without warning, so the students were strewn around the station. But it gained speed so gradually that even the slowest of us reached it and jumped aboard. The countryside was lovely, with hills and mountains just like Austria. Our spirits rose and after many hours we steamed into Belgrade. I was fascinated; the very name spoke of Cold War spies and intrigue. The timetable issued with our tickets showed an hour in Belgrade but we stayed on the same train all the way from Munich to Athens. I got out alone, leaving Margaret with our belongings.

I walked around the large Stalinist structure of Belgrade central station without being challenged so, feeling braver, left the station to get a glimpse of communist Belgrade. There were a lot of police around but no one confronted me as I left the station. I gazed at the city – or what I saw of it from the station entrance. There was a frisson of excitement to be alone behind the Iron Curtain in Belgrade but to tell the truth it looked miserable, with no colour, no shops and a muted atmosphere. The few people I saw did not raise their gaze to me and I decided to scamper back to the womb of the German train. I walked swiftly back into the station and as I got near the platform where our train had stopped I saw the end of it steaming away. Margaret would have assumed that I had got onto the train, as I often did during our stops in Yugoslavia, and work my way back to her through the carriages. The train was moving slowly but I was far too far away to reach it and the curious poignancy of the sight of the narrow end of the train steaming away from me filled me with panic.

I ran down the platform but the train by now was well out into the maze of tracks and points. There should have been plenty of time – according to my timetable the train still had twenty minutes in Belgrade and it had never left any station early. Maybe there was a time change. My mind raced away with my predicament. No ticket, no passport, no

21

money, no identity. The Yugoslavs would accuse me of spying, and Margaret would arrive in Greece alone. The whole adventure had gone badly wrong already thanks to my own stupidity. I sat on a bench in the empty platform; the station was deserted though it was only midday. I would have to give myself up shortly and hope that they believed me and shipped me out on the next train, though I knew that the Munich to Athens train only ran once a week. There were men in uniform in the station and I pondered on which to approach but I did not know what the different uniforms meant. I decided to go to the stationmaster's office, if I could find it and keep out of the way of the military, but did they speak English and finding a lone westerner on their territory wouldn't they hand me over to the military?

In those days, people who ventured across the Iron Curtain were often charged with spying just so that they had someone the communists could exchange when, inevitably, their agents were arrested in the west. It was not uncommon. They could rightly claim that I had deliberately left the German train travelling on our group transit visa. I wondered about trying to reach the Greek border on my own and to cross it but realised I would be in even bigger trouble if it went wrong, as it almost surely would. All these thoughts were going through my mind, and I cursed myself for being so stupid, when I heard a train approaching. Maybe it was a train to the west, perhaps back to Austria. It steamed in to a completely different platform, six or seven platforms away from where I was dejectedly contemplating my bleak future in a Belgrade prison. There were people waving urgently out of the window. They were waving at me. It was my train; it had returned to Belgrade station only to depart from another platform. It turned itself around so as to face the tracks to Greece. I raced over to it and fell into my compartment and Margaret's arms. The German students snorted at me and spoke in German to each other. There was no doubt what they were saying: 'Dumm Englisch'.

After a few more minutes the train again steamed out of Belgrade station and we plodded on through less interesting countryside for hours and hours. Our food supplies by now were much depleted and we were eating three-day-old bread when the train shuddered then halted at the Greek border. The Yugoslav engine was removed and the doors of the German carriages were locked. We were on the edge of a bridge over a river. The sun beat down and there was absolute silence as we slumbered in the sweltering heat in the locked, engineless train. The students grew uneasy; nothing happened for two hours. The sun began to go down and the carriage, after sitting still in the full heat, began to

22

creak and cool. I hung out of the window for air. There was a puffing and hissing from across the bridge in Greece and a small engine crossed over towards us. There were armed guards our side of the bridge. Papers were exchanged and the Greek engine coupled with us and tugged us painfully slowly across the Iron Curtain and into a Greek village, where it stopped as if exhausted.

The Greek militia unlocked the doors and we piled out into the evening air. There were people sitting in cafes, there was loud laughter, the noise of motor scooters, the aromas of good food. Our mood lifted. Although we were in Greece, a foreign country of which we knew little, we were back in the free world. That night the train, with its new Greek engine, wandered on, still at a slow pace, towards Thessaloniki which we reached late the next afternoon. Trains don't do this anymore, but oddly, it stopped there for the night and we stayed in a Greek youth hostel which, though Spartan, (after all, they invented the concept), was a relief after sleeping on the train. Next morning the train ploughed on, the passengers now punch-drunk, till it steamed in to a baking Athens and we melted into the city, oppressed by the heat. Athens was the hottest place I had ever been in my life. We took a cheap hotel and I spent a great amount of time in the shower. Almost as soon as I came out I overheated again. We were covered in mosquito bites, my leg swelled enormously and we limped to the hospital. They had seen it before. We decided to get out after a day or so and make for the islands. But we were to be delayed by a mad millionaire.

Greece: The mad millionaire (1960)

It was our first evening in Athens. We were looking for a cheap restaurant after almost a week on the train living on tins and whatever bread and fruit we bought at the stations. As Margaret and I passed an expensive-looking restaurant, we saw a large, heavily built man with, surprisingly for a Greek, a mane of blond hair. He was sitting at an outside table and he called after us: 'Are you English?' Not much English was spoken in Athens then and I turned around to look. He walked the few yards along the pavement to meet us, shook us both warmly by the hand and insisted, in fluent English, that we join him for a drink. He seemed eccentric but said he had had an English nanny. He became more and more enthusiastic about meeting us and asked where we were staying and where we planned to go. He said his name was Manolis and we must let him invite us to dinner. I said we were on our way up to see Mount Lycabettus, a famous landmark hill in Athens. 'I will take you after dinner,' he said. We ordered dinner, which to us was so fabulous that we hardly believed we were eating in such a splendid place.

The waiters were deferential towards our new friend. After dinner I thanked him for a wonderful and much unexpected evening but said we must get to our hotel as we were still tired after our long journey. 'Of course you are, of course you are,' he cried. 'I will take you back, but before that I will show you the Lycabettus.' He indicated to a waiter and handed over car keys and a few moments later a silver Citroën car appeared, one of the classic long ones with the running boards. The waiters hustled us into the rear seats; there was a driver in uniform in the front. Our new friend sat in the passenger seat and we embarked on a tour of the centre of Athens in the cooling but still tremendously hot evening. As we took off I could hardly fail to notice two things: the waiters had not slammed the doors because there weren't any, and there were no seats in the rear. Instead we were sitting on oriental carpets, which were lovely and looked expensive.

The driver took us at high speed around the centre of Athens and up to the Lycabettus. We lay on the oriental carpets with a great view because there were no doors. Strangely, it didn't feel unsafe. It was exhilarating and marvellous to see Athens at night, as if on a magic carpet, rather than trudge around after a cheap meal not knowing what was what. True to his word he took us to our hotel but when he saw it he was shocked and said we should not stay there. I insisted that this was where we were staying. He asked if we enjoyed our evening and we said enthusiastically that we had. He then said he must show us the Acropolis and other sites tomorrow and would pick us up at 9 a.m. We agreed. I did not have any feeling of misgiving; it had been a fun evening and a wonderful welcome to Greece. I knew that Greeks, rich and poor, were said to be hospitable. He was enthusiastic about us and I put it down to him being very pro-English, thanks to his nanny. It was an intolerably hot night and I hardly slept; my mosquito bites were driving me mad. The next morning up rolled the oriental conversion of a Citroën.

It was a stupendous day at the Acropolis, the museums and at lunch. Instead of having to find everything and trudge around with a map, we were chauffeured and he was an ebullient guide. Evening came and we enjoyed another delicious dinner in an expensive restaurant. We experienced such hospitality that we could never repay and thanked him warmly, saying we must go back to our hotel. Now things changed a bit. He said he would not, as a Greek, permit two lovely young English people to stay in such a dreadful hotel. He put his hand on his heart and said he would be deeply insulted if we stayed there and that we must stay with him. I demurred. He then told us that he was a younger brother, or a cousin, of Stavros Niarchos, one of the richest people in the world at the time, and we should forget about money. He would take care of everything.

I protested that we couldn't accept and that we had booked ferries to the island in three days' time. He rolled his eyes and said that if we wanted to go to the islands he would take us in his yacht. If we wanted to go to Delphi, Sparta, Olympia, the Ionian Islands, Corfu – whatever – he would take us. We only had to say. But in the meantime he refused to take us to our terrible hotel and we must stay with him. That was that. We were driven for twenty minutes to what looked in the dark to be an expensive part of Athens. We arrived at his house, the car drove into a paved area and an iron gate closed behind us. At that moment I began to understand that I had lost control.

The house was not luxurious but it was white, spacious and clean, with views over Athens. We protested that we could not stay as we had no toothbrushes and no nightclothes. These were brought by a maid and laid out on the beautiful bed we had been shown to. Now I was getting anxious but the room was deliciously cool with not a single mosquito. Next morning, downstairs, were a maid and a manservant who both spoke English, but no sign of our benefactor. They served breakfast and I made to thank them and leave. The butler said this must not happen as Mr Niarchos would be extremely upset. He was going out today but he had given orders that we should be taken wherever we wanted. I asked the butler if it was true that our benefactor was related to the Niarchos shipping family and he said it was. He hinted that our Manolis was not involved in the family shipping firm as he was too unstable and eccentric but that he was a kind man who had taken a real liking to us. He had no children and was keen for us to live with him for as long as we wanted.

Now I was getting nervous; we were becoming the toys of a very rich and slightly mad Greek. I said to the butler that we were grateful for this wonderful hospitality but we needed him to explain to our host that we must go. He said he would be in terrible trouble if we left without saying goodbye and that he had arranged a tour to Piraeus for us. I still don't know why we didn't leave there and then but I didn't know where we were. There was an ever so slight menace in the air as the butler said that of course we must do as we wished but to please stay until the evening and have dinner with Manolis before we left. The

25

chauffeur took us out and it was another great day of sightseeing, but my alarm was growing. This was a new situation for us, surrounded by wealth, taken wherever we wanted, fed lovely food, bought whatever we needed... but prisoners.

The chauffeur drove us back to the house in the evening and soon Manolis returned. He was even more enthusiastic about us living with him. 'Why not leave the English weather and live always here in Greece with me, you could have children, I will gladly look after them and you'. This was a new and worrying angle. My expression clouded; he noticed and changed the subject. Did we have a lovely day, did we need clothes, money? Shouldn't we go down to his yacht tomorrow and go to the islands? Which islands did we prefer? We played for time, let's decide tomorrow and went to bed in the same, clean, white room with fine cotton sheets. We were getting frightened. Manolis was kind and extremely hospitable, but becoming very possessive and controlling. Margaret and I hatched an escape plan. Get up early – 4 a.m. – and quietly leave the house, hoping the maid and the butler were asleep. We didn't know where we were in Athens but surely not far from a main road, safer if he chased us. It was still dark as we rose and got dressed silently, tiptoeing downstairs to the front door. I thought I might have to struggle with a complicated lock but it opened easily.

I carefully closed the large door and we stole quietly down the steps and through the front garden. Then we ran as if for our lives through the silent residential area lined with expensive houses until we came to a crossroads. There was a bus there. We somehow got to our grotty hotel, grabbed our things, checked out, got the bus to Piraeus and headed off to the islands, any island, on the first boat out. It happened to be going to Rhodes and it was here that I did something really stupid.

Greece: Hospital fourth class (1960)

They said that the interesting place to stay on Rhodes was the village of Lindos and so we rented a room there. The lady of the house had two young boys who enjoyed an idyllic life playing on the beach, on the rocks and up in the acropolis which was untended and empty apart from a few cats. I lay out on the terrace absorbing the light and the heat in a way impossible at home, where the sun was always watery. I didn't realise it was so intense and this, together with the raw elements of sea, rocks and sand, was a totally new world for me. I was in an ancient world too; every evening at mealtimes the boys' mother came onto the terrace and bawled out their names. She had no idea where they were

26

but the sound echoed over the rocks and even up to the acropolis where I was sitting one night watching the sunset. 'Pythagoras,' she shouted. 'Euclides!' Then she something else which I imagined translated to, 'Get in here! Your tea's ready!'

It was great to hear these names from antiquity still used. The intensity of the sun was new to me and I became a sun worshipper at the little house facing the beach in Lindos before there was tourism there. But after a few days of this sun worship I began to feel unwell. First I was nauseous, then extraordinarily tired, then very unwell indeed, then worse, pitifully weak. I was twenty-two, but thought I was dying in Lindos. There was no doctor but our landlady called in a local lady who knew a bit about medicine. She thought she knew at once what it was. 'You must go to the capital, Rhodes, and to the hospital. You are very ill.' I knew I was, so I told Margaret to stay there and somehow I caught the bus to Rhodes and found the hospital by asking a policeman. It turned out he spoke English, after a fashion. He wore a badge that read Tourist Police on his jacket.

He was kindly, was called Constantine, and he helped support me to get to the hospital as I could hardly walk. He almost carried me up the steps into the hospital, which was small. I think it was one of the civic buildings put up by the Mussolini government when they occupied Greece. There was a large echoing marble hall and a man sitting at a desk smoking. Constantine explained that I was a foreigner and in bad shape. He translated for me: 'They can take you. Do you want to go first class, second class, third class or fourth class?' I had no idea what it meant – I hadn't heard of different classes in a hospital. But I did know that I had practically no money. 'Fourth class, please,' I mouthed, feeling it didn't matter which class I chose as I was about to die. I slumped on a bench, unable to go further. They came with a stretcher and bumped me downstairs to a basement. It was dark but I made out ten or twelve beds, each with a patient in it. There were people sitting around each bed. Everyone fell silent as I was stretchered in.

I was put on a hard bed and Constantine stayed with me until a young doctor was summoned. He took my temperature and asked questions which Constantine translated. He called a nurse from upstairs and told her what to do with me. He then rushed upstairs as if he didn't really want to be down here in fourth class where he might catch something. The nurse laid me on the bed, put damp blankets on me and gave me water. She then disappeared. I asked Constantine in a weak whisper what was wrong with me, though I didn't care, I thought I was a goner. I was in a weaker state than I had ever imagined, my life was

27

ebbing away. 'You have a very bad case of sunstroke,' he said. 'It is dangerous. If you had not come in now you might have died as your body temperature is completely out of control.' Constantine left, but I told him about Margaret still in Lindos and he said he'd go there and bring her to Rhodes. It was part of his job, he said, to look after tourists, but there were hardly any so he had lots of time. In any case, he wanted to improve his English.

I lay there ebbing away and now that Constantine was gone the people in the fourth-class ward came over to stare at me. They offered me food but I touched nothing. The first night I stayed completely still, unable to move. Faces appeared over me to offer olives and grapes but I couldn't speak. It was dark all day down in fourth class but probably just what I needed: complete inactivity, coolness and dark. There were a lot of people, relatives of the sick, coming and going and clustering around each bed – except mine, of course. They had baskets with them and they kept coming over, sometimes in a group, looking at me as if I was an exhibit in a museum and dangling grapes, olives and bread, urging me to eat by mimicking chewing. But I couldn't.

The days passed and I vaguely wondered why I didn't see a doctor or a nurse. No one gave me any medicine nor anything to eat or drink except the offers from the relatives of the other patients. After a couple of days Constantine came back. I told him that there had been no treatment nor any food but I was beginning to feel a bit better. I said that the other patients' visitors had been taking a great deal of interest in me and were very kindly offering me food, which I didn't eat. 'Ah, you see, in fourth class they don't supply food. Your relatives must bring it. And the doctors don't come down here unless in an emergency. They are getting paid most by the people in the first class, less by those in second class and so on. They know that the people in fourth class cannot pay them much at all'. But the non-treatment in the cool dark basement worked, and after four or five days I was discharged, weak and starving.

Although I was in fourth class I still paid a daily rate; it wasn't much but I didn't have much money and now even less. Constantine brought Margaret and my things back from Lindos. He had taken to us and knew we were broke. He got us into a kind of youth hostel in the local school. Margaret and I slept on a mattress on the floor in the gymnasium. 'Why not teach English here on the island?' he said. 'Everybody wants to emigrate to America, you can earn money working a few hours in the evenings.' It sounded a good idea – and otherwise we'd have to go straight home. I was much better, but Margaret began

28

to behave as if she had a temperature. She said strange things, as if she was delirious, but it seemed to go away after a few days. Looking back, it was the first sign of what was to become a serious mental illness.

Greece: Ouzo cycling (1960)

I didn't have much money to start with, but after paying even the fourth-class rates I was much poorer. Margaret and I were both attracted to the idea of extending our stay by teaching English in the evening and having all day to explore Rhodes on hired bikes. Constantine wanted to be our first student. He said he knew of a couple who had just built a house on the edge of town. They didn't have enough money to finish it yet and were looking for a couple to rent a room. It was one of those houses where the iron rods were sticking out of the top of the roof, ready for the next level, which they couldn't yet afford. There was no working kitchen but there was a paraffin stove up on the roof and we were free to use it if we bought the oil. They had a room for us to rent which was both the bedroom and where we saw the students. Constantine would find us students and in return get free lessons. The only problem was negotiating whose turn it was to go up onto the roof and use the paraffin stove.

There was no oven in the house but down the hill there was a great communal cooking arrangement on Sundays. It was highly gender based. The women in each house took a big circular metal roasting tin, they put in it whatever they liked but mostly it was lamb (only a little, it was expensive but gave a great flavour), potatoes, aubergines, onions, tomatoes, garlic, rosemary, herbs, salt and pepper with olive oil sloshed over it. Everything was raw. Then the man of the house got on his bike and tied a strip of cloth around the circular roasting tin to form two loops from which to hang it over the handlebars. The men set off downhill to the local square, trying to stop the olive oil slopping over the tin or leaving a trail of aubergines. Down in the local square was the wood-fired bakery where the baker had just removed the last of the day's bread. We cycled over to it, formed a queue of bicycles and handed over our tin to the baker together with the bakery fee of a few drachmas.

Then came the best bit: we pushed our bikes to the village bar next door, propped them up in a long line and sat outside drinking ouzo in the sun until the baker shouted that all was ready. This took an hour or an hour and a half. Then came the tricky bit, to cycle back up the hill with a hot roasting tin over the handle bars while to a greater or lesser

29

extent smashed on ouzo. The sight of those twelve or so bicycles ridden by intoxicated Greeks, pedalling hard and weaving their way up the hill in an ill-disciplined line, Sunday roasts swinging from the handlebars, is not one I will ever forget. But it tasted marvellous, the slow roast, the wood flavour from the oven and the melting vegetables in the local olive oil. Most Sundays my new landlord Takis was one of those in the group cycling back up the hill with me.

He rode a particularly nice bike, large and sturdy, and he left the house every morning on it with a big leather satchel around his shoulders. He didn't come back until late. I asked Constantine what he did and it turned out that he was the official government collector of radio licences for Rhodes town. All day he cycled around the town banging on doors and getting the locals to cough up their radio licence fee. It was obligatory to pay this fee so he was a cycling tax collector.

Life settled down in our shared house. Margaret and I spent each day exploring and we got to use the roof stove first because our students were coming in the evenings. In any case, Takis didn't get home until late, his satchel heavy with the radio licence drachmas he had collected for the government. But there were growing tensions in the air in our house. Nearly every evening there were screeching rows coming from the other room. We heard mostly her but it was a terrible noise, a mixture of wailing and screaming with his low responses. Of course, we understood not a word but it was worrying – and difficult to get to sleep. We thought perhaps it was just the way people argue in Greece – there does seem to be a latitude effect. In Sweden or Iceland people do not seem to make so much noise in talking or in arguing as people do in Italy. Maybe, we reasoned, Greeks, being even further south, were even more volatile and loud in their language.

A few weeks later Constantine came to his usual evening class and stopped on the way in to talk to the lady of the house, who had seemed distracted and distressed lately. We didn't know why, though the constant rows were perhaps a clue. Constantine told us abruptly that we'd have to leave in two weeks as Takis was in deep trouble: they had to sell the house and he might go to prison. 'Why?' I asked. Constantine touched his nose. 'You know he collects all the money for the government for the radio licences?' Constantine lowered his voice. 'He hasn't been passing the money to the government. He has spent it all.'

Postscript. When I got home to England, the sister-in-law of my best friend said she'd like to go to Greece. She was on the rebound from a failed relationship. Did I know anyone to help her? I mentioned Constantine, the tourist policeman. She travelled to Rhodes. He was a

30

kindly man, he helped her and they quickly got married. Soon afterwards she inherited a lot of money from an unmarried aunt who she met only once or twice. Constantine became rich. He spent all the money too.

Turkey: The mental asylum (1962)

Two years passed Margaret and I had got married. We had the urge to see Greece's neighbour Turkey. It held a mysterious attraction for us because Rhodes was so close to Turkey, you saw it every time you looked out to sea. But when I asked if we could go over there the Greeks left us in no doubt that it was enemy territory; no one from Rhodes went there. Fishing boats came back with holes from gunshots if they ventured near that forbidden coast. And worse, they weren't Christian over there, they were Muslim. Don't go, they said. Of course, that made it exciting to go.

So, I resigned from the chocolate factory, where we had met, and Margaret resigned from the physics department at the university where she now worked helping to fly high altitude balloons studying the earth's radiation, and we set off from Bristol for Turkey. On our way down the steep hill from our Clifton flat to get the train to London, rucksacks laden, I passed the pub where I sometimes drank cider with the Somerset locals. Old Bert was just coming out from his lunchtime pint and game of dominoes. 'Where you off to then, my friend?' he said. Proudly, thinking Bert would find it amazingly exotic, I said, 'I'm off to Turkey, Bert.' He took this in slowly – he did drink a lot of cider. 'Oh, Torquay,' he said. 'I loves it down Torquay.'

There was another long train ride ahead, this time to Istanbul. It was a fantastic city and the Turkish food was better than the Greek. We saw the sights in Anatolia and moved to the small town of Denizli where we rented a room. But our stay took a dark turn, and we ended up in another hospital, this time a mental hospital.

I was woken at 3 a.m. by the howling of hyenas. I was asleep in a camp bed in a small side room in a Turkish mental hospital. Margaret lay, drugged, on a high hospital bed beside me. A few days earlier, after we arrived in Denizli, she became more confused and deluded than I had ever seen during a week of growing madness. It started when I became ill with fever and diarrhoea, and laid low for several days. Margaret went out to get food. My mouth was badly ulcerated and Turkish yoghurt was all I could eat. During these few days she was saying strange things. I was too ill to question it but she seemed to think

31

her thoughts were being interfered with. I didn't know it then but this is a classic symptom of a certain type of mental illness.

After five or six days I began to improve but she was becoming worse every day. As I got better I began to argue with her that what she was saying was nonsensical. She grew agitated and threw a glass on the stone floor. Of course it shattered and she became even more disturbed and lay on the glass-strewn floor in a foetal position, moaning to herself. I was getting very anxious. For the first time in my life I was dimly aware that I was dealing with a mental illness and one whose name I did not know. The landlady came up because of the noises and crashes. When she saw Margaret's condition she was as shocked as I was. I asked her where the nearest doctor was and fortunately there was one a few doors away. Together we tried to dress Margaret, who kept tearing her clothes off as soon as we tried. She was shouting, screaming, crying and swearing as we walked to the doctors, passers-by giving us a wide berth. We reached the doctors and his waiting room was completely full, but she made so much noise that he came out because of the commotion as his Turkish patients ran for it.

It was obvious that we were in deep trouble. He spoke some French and in that language told me that Madame was sick and should be taken right now to the mental hospital. There was, he said, a small one on the edge of the town. He called a taxi and came with us. It took only fifteen minutes to get to the gaunt building on a rocky point overlooking the sea but Margaret fought with amazing strength. When we got to the small hospital she became supernaturally strong, and it took three or four male nurses to control her. They took her to a side room and closed the door. She smashed the window with her bare fists and her wrist began to pour blood. They held her down and put four or five stitches in her wrist. The senior doctor joined us and sat quietly in the room with us for ten minutes. He spoke some English and asked her a few questions – such as her name, her age – but she was completely and violently crazed. She hit out even with her injured hand. She screamed, got onto the bed and then collapsed into a catatonic trance, covered in blood from her reopened wound.

I was heartbroken, horrified, shocked and frightened. I had never seen anything like this in anyone, let alone my lovely new wife. The doctor motioned for me to leave with him and we left two strong male nurses, who dodged plates, glasses and yoghurt, to try to clean her up and calm her. Outside it was getting dark. The doctor said, as if I hadn't guessed it by now, that my wife was seriously mentally ill and we should return to Britain as soon as they could make her stable enough to travel. I asked him what on earth was wrong and how could it have happened. Either he did not want to tell me or his English was not up to it but he said that the doctors in England would explain the illness to me. The only treatment that might stabilise her was strychnine, he said. I had heard of it but I thought it was a poison. I said so but he didn't seem to understand. He said there was also electric shock treatment. He asked me what I wanted to do.

I didn't want either treatment for her but the situation was impossible; we could not get home like this. I did not fancy letting her have electric shock treatment in a poorly equipped Turkish mental hospital but he said the strychnine injections should calm her symptoms down enough to leave for home in, say, a week. I slept in the room with her and she was calm until early morning but then the violent behaviour started again. I tried to eat breakfast with her but everything was smashed and thrown around the room. I was sick with worry so had not the slightest appetite, though my ulcerated mouth was improving. The nearest town with a British Consulate was Antalya.

I took a four-hour bus ride there as I knew we would not to be able to get home with our return rail tickets. We had to fly. I had never flown. The consul was a Turkish businessman and was helpful as I explained the whole story. He shook his head gravely through a cloud of Turkish tobacco smoke. He got out the forms that had to be filled in to allow him, on behalf of the British Government, to pay my fare home. He said he would advance the money for the airfare but had to mark our passports as being valid only for the one-way trip home, after which they became invalid until I repaid the money. I took the cash and walked to the nearest office of Turkish Airlines to book a flight to London in four days' time. There was a small plane that left for Istanbul at 5 a.m. and there a transfer to a British Airways flight to London, which stopped briefly in Athens en-route.

Once this was arranged, I took the slow trip back to the mental hospital with an aching heart. How was I to get Margaret home unless she improved a lot? They were kind in the mental hospital and did what they could but I slept every night in the same room with her and most nights got little sleep. That lack of sleep, added to the high anxiety about our situation, led me to feel very upset and sad, but I knew there was a major task ahead. I longed for the arrival in Heathrow where Margaret could be admitted to a British hospital. As the strychnine treatment progressed Margaret did become more and more sedated. I was scared stiff at what it might be doing to her, but there was no other way to get home, and it was a million times better than the violent rages.

On the third day she recognised me again and sat up. She suddenly became loving and gentle with me. It was hard to handle after the madness but, of course, it gave me hope. I kissed her and she kissed me back sensually. She opened her mouth and it seemed like a nice, loving kiss – we were, after all, still newlyweds. She coaxed my tongue inside her mouth. I was uneasy but overjoyed that this might be the first steps back to the girl I knew and loved and to her sanity. As we kissed I looked in her eyes and saw her gazing into mine. It was lovely, she was recovering. Suddenly, her eyes glazed, she bit down on my tongue, hard. I cried out in terrible pain and the nurses rushed in.

I didn't explain what had happened to me and didn't want to. The next few days were draining. Even the staff who spoke a little English said they did not understand what she was saying. In truth, nor did I. She talked of the doctors interfering with her thoughts; she said there was an evil eye on her; she drew pictures of huge forbidding eyes. One minute she said she was Joan of Arc and the next she was 'Peggy'. I tried, in her lucid periods, to understand what might have triggered this violent breakdown in her personality. It was clear that poor Margaret was unaware that there was anything wrong with her. On the contrary, she spoke convincingly of what had happened. It was me, she asserted, who had become ill and she had had to bring me to this hospital where she was looking after me. She said, though, that she had had enough of it and was leaving at once. She meant it: she jumped off the bed and took off out of the tiny room and down the corridor. She sprinted out of the door and down the front steps to the rocky coast on which the hospital stood.

I shouted out and rushed after her with several nurses on my heels. Despite the strychnine she was possessed of maniacal speed and strength. Margaret tore along through the rocky headland in a nightdress and we stumbled after her as if in a Swedish avant-garde film. She fell and we caught up and managed to restrain her. All the way back along the cliff to the hospital she let out blood-curdling screams, until another shot of strychnine was delivered. I didn't sleep a wink. How could we make the trip home? The doctor said the only hope was to keep her drugged as heavily as was safe for the whole journey. He would give me strychnine in tablet form but she had to be able to walk and answer questions otherwise she may not be let through. It was going to be a terribly fine balance.

34

The last two nights I got no sleep; Margaret was quieter thanks to the drugs, but the other patients groaning and jabbering kept me awake, as did my own terrors. I was twenty-two and had never experienced anything in my life like the last ten days. Each night, in the darkness, the Anatolian hyenas gathered around the hospital and howled as if in competition with the inmates. But they were never seen. Sometimes I got to sleep by morning, but then the muezzin called the faithful to prayer, and the sounds merged in a mad alien cacophony. The day of our journey arrived. The doctor gave Margaret a shot of strychnine in the middle of the night and gave me a supply of tablets. We left at 2 a.m. to get the flight from Antalya. It was dark as the taxi arrived and she slept all the way to the tiny airfield. She was fortunately still drowsy as we boarded the small plane and the few other passengers took little notice at that time of day.

The small plane lifted off for Istanbul and, despite my acute anxiety, I felt a thrill as, for the first time in my life, I left the ground, the Anatolian landscape dropping away as the sun rose. As we reached the clouds I prayed that soon we would be home. There were so many questions on my mind as we levelled off. How could my beautiful young wife, an intelligent and clever girl, turn into this violent and crazed person that I had spent the last ten days with? What caused it? I thought that perhaps the experience of rural Turkey was so different, so disorientating for her that it temporarily unhinged her mind. I thought maybe our diet had been poor. Maybe the strangeness of a situation robbed a person of their reason. As we sped towards Istanbul, where we had spent happy days at the beginning of our trip, I convinced myself that all would return to normal when we got home, and this would seem like a bad dream. I was wrong.

We landed at Istanbul and it was a couple of hours before the flight to London left. The planes were, I think, called Viscounts, and were not as fast as today's planes, and in any case there was a stop in Athens, so we would not get to London till evening. Margaret was becoming more lively and agitated, staring around at the airport. She had never flown before either. I thought I should administer the first of my small stock of strychnine tablets. She made a big fuss taking them and the noise caused consternation among the other passengers. In those days there were only a few passengers in each airport; they were quiet and exclusive places used mainly by businessmen and the wealthy. By the time we boarded the aircraft even the ground staff were disconcerted and asked me what was wrong. I explained and they said they needed to

35

speak to the captain; the other passengers looked nervous. I was asked to go up to the cockpit.

I grabbed a letter from the Turkish hospital, which said that she was very ill and needed to get home. The doctor stated that in his opinion Margaret was well enough to travel home if she took the medication. The Turkish ground staff translated this to the captain who then said he'd come back to take a look. Thanks to my earlier administration Margaret was drowsy and apart from incoherent mumblings she did not appear to be any threat. He nodded to me returned to the cockpit and we took off for Athens. She slept all the way until we landed at Athens where we were all asked to stay on board while new passengers joined us. During our ground stop she wanted to go to the toilet. I took her there and stood outside, my heart in my mouth. She was in there a long time.

The passengers going from Athens to London boarded, the aircraft doors were closed and we were asked to return to our seats for take-off. I knocked on the toilet door and spoke quietly through it, imploring her to come out. This made it worse. She started to scream and shout, banging heavily on the walls and door of the toilet. Margaret would not come out. By now the new crew and the passengers were showing signs of anxiety, but not as much as I was feeling. The crew fetched a master key to open the toilet and Margaret emerged, haggard and belligerent. She sat down and I tried to give her more tablets. But even while I was fumbling for them I was called up again to the cockpit.

It was a different captain but the previous one had obviously talked to him. He said they would not take us to London as she posed a threat to the security of the passengers and the aircraft. We had to get off, he said, it was too dangerous to take us. I pleaded. I said that if we got the strychnine into her she would calm down. I knew we were now only four or five hours from home, where help was waiting. I told them what a desperate position we would be in if they did not take us. But they were adamant and I suppose one can see why. We would be taken off and the airline would take us in a couple of days, on the next flight to London, if I got a Greek doctor's certificate that she was fit to travel and if she did not repeat the behaviour in the toilet. The aircraft doors were reopened and we were trundled off into Athens airport. My heart sank. I had little money and was close to despair.

They gave me our bags and we passed through Greek Immigration and Customs. The Greek immigration officer had trouble with her passport and asked her name. 'Winston Churchill,' she replied without hesitation. I managed to feed her two more pills but they did not seem strong enough to have much effect and the injection must now have worn off. Margaret was, in any case, now convinced that I was trying to poison her. I found a cheap hotel near the airport to wait the two days and convince a doctor to write a letter certifying that Margaret was not a danger to others and to the aircraft. I also needed him to supply me with more strychnine.

The hotel was not too keen on accepting us when they saw her, suggesting that a hospital was a more appropriate place to stay. I eventually persuaded them that she would be OK if we got a doctor and so they sent for one who spoke English. In the languid Greek way he smoked several cigarettes while talking to me and trying to communicate with Margaret. He was not convinced that she was safe to travel and proposed that I should take her to the Athens mental hospital. I said that we had already been in a Turkish mental hospital and that the only thing that might put her right was to get home. He wrote out a certificate stating that he had examined her and with medication she was fit to travel. As he gave it to me he sighed and shook his head. He was happier once he had charged me an exorbitant fee and left.

The next day passed in a dream. I watched Margaret like a hawk and gave her more tablets if I saw any signs of high activity developing, but it was a continual fight of cajoling, akin to persuading a cat to take a tablet. She would hold it under her tongue for ages and then spit it out. I did not sleep, fearing what would happen if we were rejected again. I had no money now. On the morning of the flight I got the tablets in before she was fully awake. At the airport she announced that she was 'Queen Margaret' but no one was interested. We boarded the aircraft and I was again in a high state of anxiety. The crew knew we had been turned away two days before and asked me for the doctor's certificate. This again was translated for the captain by the ground staff. The crew kept a close eye on her but thanks to the near overdose of pills she was sound asleep. The captain came out, reassured by the peaceful situation.

She only woke upon landing at Heathrow. A wheelchair came to the aircraft and after we cleared customs we came out to find her parents waiting. They had waited for two days. They must have been shocked. We got into the car but she was getting active again and I had no more pills. We stopped at a café and Margaret ran off again but eventually we did get home. I called the GP who contacted the mental hospital outside Bristol. We took her there that night. It was a forbidding old Victorian asylum and she was to stay there for more than two months. I visited a day or so later and she was even worse than in Turkey. To my horror they constrained her in a straitjacket, something I had heard of but never

37

seen. They said it was because she kept running away into the December night with nothing on. Even strong sedatives had no effect but they did not use strychnine, which they said was a primitive treatment. She was again unnaturally strong.

Margaret's mother and I were called into the matron's office and her mother stood on a small oval rug on the polished floor. Margaret was brought in; she took one look at her mother, she bent down to floor level and gave the rug a violent tug. Mother was literally swept off her feet and hit the deck. Margaret ran out, tearing off her clothes, and four nurses chased after her, just like on the cliffs in Turkey, but this time into the cold Somerset night. She was dragged back in making strange noises and screams, her eyes glazed as if she saw nothing. The senior consultant came in, a quiet pensive Scot with the air of having seen everything the world had thrown at him. Margaret was removed and the rug straightened. He turned to me. 'Do you understand what is wrong with your wife?' he said. 'No, I don't,' I replied, 'but of course I want to know what it is and how it has happened. It has been a terrifying time for both of us. What is the treatment? Do you think she can recover?'

'I'm afraid there is no cure,' he said. 'Your wife has schizophrenia.' Each syllable hit me like a hammer. I had heard of it – it seemed to be linked to the idea of a split personality. But I had never heard of or met anyone who had it. I asked if she would get better. The senior consultant said she would very likely recover after six weeks or so in the hospital, but that there was no cure, and it would probably recur. 'We can sometimes alleviate the symptoms with electroconvulsive therapy.' It made me wince just to think of applying an electric current to my lovely young wife's brain. He saw I was shocked; my new wife had, in ten days, transmogrified from a youthful, attractive, bright, hardworking and loving girl into a gaunt, violent and unpredictable woman who heard voices, smashed her hands through glass doors, said her thoughts were being interfered with and had become classically insane.

I needed to grasp at a straw. 'Do you think this is a one-off attack triggered perhaps by our trip to remotest Turkey?' I pleaded. 'I can't be certain of the prognosis,' he said. 'There are cases where it never recurs and since your wife has not suffered an attack before there is that possibility. But this is a severe case and I'm afraid I can only guess that it will recur.'

My whole married life and my future, as I sat in that mental hospital just before Christmas, looked bleak. I had no job and a severely mentally ill wife whose affliction might be permanent. I had no money.

'What can I do to deal with this?' I said, quietly but desperately, more to myself than to him. He looked down at the still rumpled rug, and then at my mother–in-law, who had said nothing. He sighed again and looked out at the black December afternoon. 'I'm afraid you will need infinite patience and infinite understanding if you are to survive yourself.'

How could my life have got into this difficulty so early in my adulthood and after so many tough years of work and study to get even as far as I had. I left the asylum in a fog of misery and despair.

Bristol: Intermolecular Forces (diamonds from peanut butter) (1963)

We were back in Bristol but I had no job. Thanks to all the part tine study I did hold the equivalent of a degree in chemistry, though I had never been to university. Margaret was still in the mental hospital. I got a job in a local department store called Maggs, near the university. I was the man in the brown coat unloading the goods from the lorries and taking them around the store in a large square basket on wheels. The basket was padded with carpet around the edges to minimise damage when cornering, as it was almost impossible to steer. It was exciting, like Christmas, unwrapping parcels every day. I never knew where I was off to next, perhaps to Babyland or Toyland or the haberdashery or, if I was lucky, to the beautiful assistants in the lingerie department.

The only man they ever saw there, one with wheels and an impressive turn of speed, was me. I liked to think I was their knight in shining armour, me in my brown overall swiftly delivering pink brassieres, petticoats and black suspender belts. I didn't know what to do next but I reminded myself that, despite my domestic problems with a very sick wife, I did have a scientific qualification after those years of cycling to night school. One lunchtime I nipped out to buy a sandwich, passing the chemistry department of the university. On an impulse, I entered the building. The secretary was there. 'Is the professor in?' I asked. She looked suspicious. 'Does he know you?' 'No, but I was wondering about doing research here?' She melted a bit. Was it my brown warehouse coat, which I hadn't removed as I had only planned to go out for a few minutes?

The professor was a polite academic, sitting at his desk and finishing his own sandwich, hastily brushing away the crumbs. He looked startled. Who was this man barging in at lunchtime and why was he wearing a brown overall with the name of a local department store on the front? I explained that I had the equivalent of a chemistry degree from the Royal Institute of Chemistry through many years of part-time study at night school. Now it was time to do real research, preferably in the field of physical chemistry. He looked me up and down. Fortunately, I hadn't brought the basket on wheels with me but I am sure I appeared to be not a budding scientist but someone employed at a junior warehousing level in the retail industry who had just walked in off the street. I confirmed, when asked, that I had never been to a university. He seemed nevertheless fascinated: this was out of the ordinary.

He stared at me and my brown coat. He was hesitant, but eventually said, 'Well, if you do have the qualification you say you have it so happens I do have a grant available for a PhD post which was not taken up by the recipient. 'What is the subject?' I asked. 'It is to study and try to increase our knowledge of intermolecular forces between unlike molecules,' he said. 'That would be fine,' I blurted out, having not the slightest idea how or why you would do such a thing. My supervisor was a senior lecturer, an Australian who, naturally, was called Bruce. He said I would have to build a gas chromatograph to work at high pressures to study what happened when unlike molecules interacted at such pressures. They would give me a room in the basement under the stairs in case I blew myself up. There was a theory about these interactions, which involved a concept called virial coefficients. Don't even think of looking it up; it starts like this.

$$\Xi = \sum_n \lambda^n Q_n = e^{(pV)/(k_B T)}$$

Nobody had been able to examine whether the theory was correct at high pressures. My job was to do the experiments to prove or disprove the theory. Those who know a little of science will know that this is the way it works. A scientific theory is developed, but it is just that, a theory. Then, it is usually another scientist who constructs the experiments in real life to see if things behave as the theory has predicted. If they do, the theory is correct and can be safely used to predict how other things will behave in other conditions. If they don't, then it is the theory that is wrong, not the natural world, and the theory then must be discarded or modified.

I spent two and a half years building the high-pressure equipment and got all my experimental results in the last six months. Bruce was splendidly eccentric and came down to my basement cell from time to time, smoking a big cigar. He loved the idea of high pressures. I don't know if this was to excite me about high pressure but he kept telling me that if we used a sufficiently high pressure we could make diamonds from anything containing carbon. He was insistent that it was possible to start with peanut butter. Diamonds from peanut butter. But, perhaps unwisely, as I might have become a rich diamond producer and a major importer of peanut butter, I stuck to using the high-pressure equipment to study intermolecular forces and virial coefficients.

Swansea: Thin cyclist on tramp steamer (1966)

I now had a PhD in thermodynamics, a branch of physical chemistry. But I was broke and by now had a little girl, Suzie, who was a few weeks old. Thanks to Yuri Gagarin, the Russian astronaut, I was on a tramp steamer leaving Swansea to go to America. I will always be grateful to Yuri – not that we ever met – because when he was launched into space it caused panic in the US. How was it that their enemies in a country like Russia had achieved this while the US was not even in the race? It was humiliating. Their answer was to throw a lot of new money at scientific research. I was a newly minted PhD and received six offers from the US. I took the one in California.

The tramp steamer was called Bristol City, a cargo vessel owned by a small shipping company called Charlie Hill. The locals called them Charlie Hill's submarines because no one knew how they managed to get to the US and no other ship ever reported seeing them en-route. The Bristol City took only five passengers. The fare was £64 from Bristol to New York, but the ticket said that they might leave from Bristol or anywhere else in the south-west, and you had to get yourself there. Two days before departure they told me we were leaving from Swansea Docks. California was to be our home for at least two years and I thought I'd better take what we needed, including cutlery, clothes, bedding and cooking utensils. I took lots of nappies for Suzie, who was only three months old. I even packed apples in case scurvy attacked during the crossing or the food was inadequate. I bought a huge trunk and we filled it. I could not lift it alone but we somehow got it in the car and to Swansea docks.

This was before the age of containers, and the Bristol City was the scene of great activity, with cranes dropping all shapes and sizes of cargo into the hold. Dockers carrying boxes and bags swarmed over the vessel and a couple of the crew came down the gangplank and carried my trunk up as if it were a toy. They dumped it in my cabin where it occupied most of the floor space. There were four other passengers: a quiet married, retired couple who were making the sea trip a holiday; an American lady returning home after a stay in Europe; and a thin, wiry, almost emaciated Englishman who pushed his bicycle up the gangplank and told me he was cycling around the world. The bike was strung up in a locker with hawsers and oil cans and the Bristol City set sail. They told me it would take a week to New York but they didn't guarantee it. Still, I thought, they must feed you three meals a day so they'll want to avoid too much delay.

The cabin was clad in dark brown wood but much better than I had expected. With so few passengers, we and the officers ate together in the dark brown wood dining room. A steward walked along the corridor ringing a bell at meal times and we assembled on the dot. The man with the bicycle always sat next to me. On the night of our first dinner, we were just heading out around Ireland. The boat was rocking a bit but nothing serious. They served Brown Windsor soup. The cyclist looked at it intently, as if it contained an inner meaning or it puzzled him. He continued to do this as the rest of us started our soup. He said nothing but shortly he stood up and left the room without touching his soup. He did not return until breakfast the next day, when precisely the same thing happened. It was to happen regularly three times a day for the whole of the voyage.

He never missed a mealtime. He appeared punctually at the call of the bell, was served his food, stared at it for a few minutes and then left. If he was thin and wiry when we left Bristol, he was as thin as his bicycle when we passed the Statue of Liberty. Everyone else ate most of the time though we lost our appetites in the huge seas that were to come. It was the North Atlantic, it was April, when gales are common, and it was a small boat. I was the youngest at the table and the captain, a cheery Devonian with a naval beard, liked to talk politics. I was a man without any financial resources, having just completed a PhD. Indeed, I was broke. I championed universal free education, the National Health Service and the like. The captain teased me going to the land of the capitalists and assured me I would not get along too well in America with such left-wing views.

I did not think it was terribly left wing to favour equal access to education and health care but I knew little of America and was to find the NHS a source of discussion there, with Americans who called it 'socialised medicine'. I soon discovered Americans strongly believed that the private sector did things most efficiently and that the wasteful government should be kept out of everything, except for a few things like law and order and foreign affairs. They were convinced that the British government allocated each citizen a doctor and it was dictatorial, cheap and nasty. I defended equality in health and education but when I saw the health care in the US I realised they had a point, though I saw the term 'socialised medicine' as a bit of an insult passed on by the American Medical Association to make sure they didn't lose their large salaries. They didn't like me pointing out that Yuri Gagarin's feat had been achieved by the government of the USSR.

We sailed on, saying 'hello' three times a day to the cyclist. The seas got steeper and steeper. It brought to mind a picture of a boat from school. As a kid I painted a row of waves along the bottom of the picture in a nice line and coloured them blue. On top of these waves sat a boat – black, white or grey – and on top of the boat was a big funnel with smoke coming out. In my childish pictures the boat was a lot bigger than the waves. But as we headed out of the protection of Ireland into the raw Atlantic it became rather different. Now, as I stood at the back of the boat, I saw huge heaving hillocks of grey water with spray blowing off them; the Bristol City was a speck climbing up these spitting hills, overbalancing at the top with the engines screaming as the propeller came out of the water and then charging down the other side of the hill of seawater with a sickening thud at the bottom as if we had hit the ocean floor. I had always thought of stairs as leading from somewhere lower up to somewhere higher. Now I found that the stairs sometimes led up and sometimes down. It changed in seconds.

Every day the navigator pinned up a map showing how far we were and he began to admit that due to the sea conditions we were not going to do it in a week. Every day we put our clocks back half an hour. It wasn't jet lag but I couldn't concentrate. I resolved to read up on the science in preparation for my new job and there were a dozen paperbacks novels in the trunk, but the constant motion sapped my will. After four or five days we heard Newfoundland on the radio and then saw it grey and wet through the spray. America, at last! I didn't realise that we were only halfway. One fine day – I thought it would never come, it was the eleventh day – we steamed up through the Narrows and there stood the island of Manhattan. I pictured us landing outside the Empire State Building. The navigator chuckled, 'No, we go right past it and upriver to Port Elizabeth.'

I wasn't to see New York for a further two years, on the way home. My heart sank as we moved past Manhattan, the landscape became more and more sleazy until finally we tied up in Port Elizabeth, a grim, rundown port you wouldn't want to find yourself alone in on a dark night with a heavy trunk. It was too late to do anything by the time Customs and Immigration came on board. They passed me for entry but disallowed my remaining three apples, which had to be returned to UK or more likely dumped at sea. Although it was almost dark the thin cyclist perked up, took down his bicycle from the chain room, put a huge pannier on the back, wheeled it down the gangplank and wobbled off into the night on his now pin-like frame. I gave him the university address in California, 3000 miles away, and he said he would drop in. It looked as if he was more likely to drop off as he disappeared into the murk of the Port Elizabeth warehouses and cheap bars.

In the morning, ashore I phoned for a taxi. When it arrived the crew put the trunk in the boot. The boot wouldn't close but we bumped along the docks to the Greyhound bus station. We could hardly lift the trunk out of the boot and we could not move it far, so the taxi driver and I set it down on what I was to learn to call the sidewalk. It was so heavy I thought no one could steal it and I entered the terminal to have a coffee and kill an hour before the bus left for Chicago – my next stop. This was my first contact with America – a bus station in Port Elizabeth. The cafeteria was brightly lit, as if for medical operations. There was stainless steel and neon lighting. On display were enormous pieces of cake and tart. Each piece disappeared beneath white waves of cream, and the fruit spilling out onto the side of the plate was so brightly coloured I didn't believe it was real

The staff seemed to be in a hurry for my order. I was harassed by the pressure to decide and all the options they gave me for the coffee but I took my Technicolor tart and a large mug of coffee and sat under the neon glow. The food tasted sugary and scented. I soon found that everything, even the bread and the cheese, had this flavour. The Greyhound bus arrived and the driver and I lifted the trunk into it. We set off through the wastelands of Port Elizabeth and emerged onto the 'Turnpike'. I'd never seen such a highway. We drove along and every two hours stopped at different cafeterias. But they were all the same as the one in Port Elizabeth, bathed in neon with identical fruit tarts submerged in cream. Everything still tasted sweet, even the beef sandwich.

The Greyhound bus, like a horse being watered, had unmanned hoses stuck into it for fuel and then we drove on again for two more hours until stopping at another identical cafeteria. The terrible uniformity of Middle America came to me and I became depressed at the prospect of spending a couple of years there. It took twenty-seven hours to get to Chicago. Various people sat next to me on the bus as we stopped at Philadelphia, Grand Rapids and so on. I was struck by their friendliness and openness. They talked about things that, in the UK, would never be broached with a stranger: how much they made a month; the state of their marriage; what they thought of their boss; their politics. But some of them seemed nutty or even half crazy to me and I was puzzled by it all.

Reunited in Chicago with Margaret and our three-month old daughter, Suzie, they had flown there, we were ready for the last leg of the overland journey – the Santa Fe train. The train stood in Chicago station as if it was a set for a musical. The attendants, who were black, wore white uniforms and white gloves and stood by each carriage door with little steps to get you up. I thought they might start to tap dance as we boarded. After the Greyhound Bus it was a luxury liner with our own room and beds made up at night. Dining was in a large plastic dome. To have a big steak and half an iceberg lettuce (I hadn't seen one before) was wonderful. The steaks were ten times the size of what we might have expected in mid-1960s Britain. Things were looking good.

After Laramie and Cheyenne, we were into mountains and deserts and as I sat in the dome rounding through such beautiful scenery and eating such good, fresh food and such generous portions my spirits rose. America was not all the same. Even the people out here in the west were more fun.

California: A bungalow in Pacific Palisades (1966)

I had travelled from Swansea to Santa Monica, 5307 miles, every inch of the journey over the Earth's surface. Thanks to the Russian lead in the space race, funds for research in physics and chemistry were flooding into the universities, and I had a new job at the University of California. They wanted me to continue with my high-pressure chromatography. 'The Windsors, I presume,' said Professor Bob Pecsok as I struggled with the trunk at Los Angeles Union Station. He was a big, confident chap, instantly friendly, who had offered me the post. Bob and I not met; how did he know it was us? Perhaps my thick flannel trousers, Margaret's National Health glasses and our British winter pallor gave it away.

The Californians were big, suntanned, oozing good health and with very white teeth. I felt unhealthy just looking at them. We sped off along Sunset Boulevard for the twenty-mile drive to Santa Monica, alongside the Pacific Ocean, after struggling with the trunk. Why did I bring saucepans and a kettle? Did Suzie really need so many nappies?

45

Didn't they have them in California? Should I just dump it on Sunset Boulevard? I wasn't sure if they had booked an apartment or a hotel for us to start our stay. Bob turned to me. 'My mother's away in Texas. You can stay in her house until you find somewhere.' We rolled into Pacific Palisades, on a cliff above Santa Monica, to a charming bungalow overlooking the ocean. 'Make yourselves at home. There's oranges growing in the yard, bacon and eggs and beer in the fridge and a Ford Fairlane in the garage,' said Bob.

He lived nearby and invited us to dinner the next night. It was a fantasy life after 1960s Britain. Just as Bob said, there were oranges growing on trees in the garden, bacon and eggs in the fridge and a Ford Fairlane with whitewall tyres in the garage. The bungalow had one strange feature: the mailbox slot was set into the front wall – but not near the main door, which was at the side of the house, but into our bedroom. Not only that, but it was directly over the bed. Every morning as we heard the postman walking up the path we had to duck, weave and move fast. Parcels from England were a danger and could knock you out before you even woke up.

Apart from that it was paradise, with the sun shining every day and the Pacific Ocean just down the street. Bob took me into the university each day for the first week but LA was no place to be without a car and so one evening I got Bob's mother's Ford Fairlane out of the garage. I had only just passed my test in Britain and I never owned a car. This 1957 Fairlane sported a white body that went on forever, a gold stripe halfway up and a light blue top. The back ended in huge fins and taillights like something from a fun fair. It was an automatic, I had never driven one before, and I gingerly took it down the road.

It was a huge vehicle but it drove well in straight lines, not so well on curves. I turned onto Pacific Coast Highway. The ocean was gold and red in the setting sun, it was hard to see along the gleaming bonnet. High on the thrill of driving a two-tone, whitewall-tyred monster along the Pacific coast I was slow to notice the lack of petrol. I pulled into a Chevron station. I remembered it was 'gas' rather than 'petrol' and avoided the word. 'Fill her up, please,' I said to the attendant, who was wearing a flat white hat, like a sailor's hat but with the word 'Chevron' emblazoned across the front.

He disappeared, plugged in the pump and reappeared to wash the windscreen and check the oil. He came back and told me the price, and I paid. I tried to start the Ford Fairlane. Just a dead clicking sound. My first trip out in Bob's mother's car and here I was, stuck. I didn't fancy phoning Bob – perhaps he hadn't meant me to take the car out and was just being nice. I was blocking the pump. Chevron-man came over: 'Whassa madder, bud?' he drawled. 'It won't start, the battery is flat,' I explained. 'Scuse me, I don't folla ya.' I said it more clearly. 'I think the batt-e-ry is flat.' 'What d'ya mean?' I said it again. 'Wait a minute,' he said. He raced off and brought his colleague over. 'Say it again,' he said, and they both stared at me with their Chevron hats almost touching.

'My b-a-t-t-e-r-y is f-l-a-t. I enunciated each syllable to make it clear, and said it twice more. Do they come from Mars? I thought. Don't they speak English? Suddenly a beam of recognition spread over the face of the colleague. 'His baddery's dead!' Relieved at this sudden breakthrough, I soon learnt to turn the t's into d's and ask where the 'budder' was in the supermarket. I learnt that they didn't understand the word 'fortnight', it wasn't wise to ask for a 'rubber' in the office, they were obliged to say 'you're welcome' every single time you said 'thank you', you drove on the pavement and walked on the sidewalk and that 'how are you?' did not mean they wanted to know how you were.

I found them generous and hospitable, though trouble was looming for us. It was refreshing how efficient it all was. This new country worked better than my old one but everyone seemed to be in a hurry. For my work at the university I needed a gauge to measure high pressures. I had also needed one in Bristol for my PhD work but I waited six months for the firm in Manchester to produce it and deliver it to Bristol so I was apprehensive about how long it took here, especially as the only firm making such instruments was 2000 miles away in Chicago. I phoned them and explained exactly what I needed, and asked if they made a high-pressure gauge to that specification. 'Yessiree, we sure do.' 'I am in a bit of a hurry for it as I am not sure how long I will have here,' I said. There was a short silence, a calculation. 'Sir, I can't get it to you today but you can have it at UCLA tomorrow morning.'

Bob Pecsok frequently invited us to his house nearby for dinner. After dinner he always showed us slides of Britain as if we had never been there. I spent hours in Pacific Palisades making admiring noises about Strafford-on-Avon. But fortunately in recompense he made the strongest gin and tonics I have ever sipped. One was plenty but he always pressed you to have two. A year into our stay my parents came out to California to visit. Mother had never been abroad and neither of them drank alcohol, due to their Methodist upbringing.

Bob invited us all over for a barbecue and when we got there suggested that my parents might like to have a gin and tonic, under the impression that all Brits drank G&Ts all the time. I don't think my parents knew what a G&T was but they both accepted. He brought out the drinks. My father sipped it, evidently liked it very much, and drank it in four minutes. Bob was pleased to see this and brought him another which he also downed. Mother drank hers more slowly. She evidently liked it but she began to turn bright red and giggle whenever Bob said anything. I hadn't seen her like this before; she was usually restrained. Meanwhile Dad, with two strong G&Ts inside of him, was getting familiar and amorous with Bob's wife, Mary. It was time to get them out of there and into the Ford Fairlane before I was fired.

California conversations (1966)

The first supermarket

The size of the supermarkets and the range of goods, the choice, was staggering. I needed a lot of things, food and so on, to establish our new home in Pacific Palisades. When my trolley was full I headed to the checkouts and over one I saw a banner reading 'CASHIER OF THE MONTH'. That's the one for me, I thought, she will be helpful with my very first transaction in California, our new home. There was one customer in front of me. He moved up to her till and she glanced at him. 'Hi, how are you, what nice teeth you've got,' she said, showing her own in a quick smile. 'Gee, thanks, appreciate it,' he said. This must be what made her Cashier of the Month, she found something nice to say to each customer.

Of course, I didn't know if it was always going to be dental, but my teeth were in terrible condition, as I had not looked after them at all when I was an impoverished student. I sucked at them feverishly while she was calling out and tapping his prices into the till. There were no scanners then, the cashiers read the price label out loud on every item and typed in the amount. I had put toothpaste in my trolley but it would have taken more than that and there wasn't time before checkout to get my teeth into shape. What would she say to me, and would she lose the accolade of Cashier of the Month if she didn't come up with anything nice? It could not be a dental compliment in my case.

I brushed down my hair and composed a smile with my mouth shut tight as my turn arrived and we faced each other. I tried to say hello through pursed lips – which is tricky, try it. She looked at me closely for a split second. She paused, her mind working hard on it but evidently not coming to any resolution on something nice to say. It was hurtful. She said only, 'Hi, how are you? 1.99, 2.66, 3.99.'

Remarkably good English

Three scientists, one each from Scotland, New Zealand and Australia, arrived to work in the chemistry department at UCLA just after me. I was the only one that owned a car, the magnificent Ford Fairlane with whitewall tyres. They were looking for an apartment to share and asked me to drive them around a few apartments available in Santa Monica one evening. At one of them a large woman with huge hair and a broad Texan accent showed us around. They liked the apartment and she appeared to like them. They said they were interested and talked to her about the apartment and what was included, and then they agreed a price.

We were just leaving when she said, 'Hey, where're y'all from?' The New Zealander replied, 'I'm from New Zealand, he's from Scotland and he's from Australia.' She brightened. 'That's fantastic, I am so impressed,' she said. We didn't quite know what was so impressive about being from these three countries but she was about to tell us. 'Yeah, I am so impressed. Y'all speak English so well.'

Californian wine

A week or so after arriving I ventured out to eat for the first time. It was, admittedly, a rather cheap restaurant in LA. Having wine at home had been a rarity, only for Christmas and wedding anniversaries, but here it was cheap and the wine industry was growing fast in the state. I was interested to see what kind of wine they were making and now suddenly I now had money to have wine with food. The waiter, a typical young Californian – fit, tanned, lovely teeth – came over to take our order. There was one local red wine on the menu but it gave no details of it or of vintage etc.

I said to him, 'I would be interested to try this red wine, do you know anything about it, what year it is, how old it is?' He no doubt picked up that I was a foreigner from my accent. There was a long pause as he considered this odd request suspiciously. But I sensed he wanted to reassure me. He chose his words carefully. 'Sir, you don't need to worry about that, all our wine is fresh.'

At the Disneyland Hilton, Los Angeles

A Scottish family I knew were visiting California and staying at the Sheraton, Disneyland, where I had a drink with them. We were sprawled on deep sofas in the bar: Mum who was in her fifties and widowed, her twenty-eight-year-old daughter, the daughter's eight-year-old son Bruce, and Mum's long-term partner, Norman, who was a few years younger than her. They all lived together in Peebles in Scotland. Bruce's father had disappeared just after he was born but Norman had always been there. Bruce grew up living in Gran's house but thinking Norman was his father and he called him Dad. It worked well and the adults all found it best to keep it that way.

As we talked about their visit, there was an American couple at the next sofa who overheard the conversation and seemed eager to join in. 'Gee, I love your Scottish accents,' the man said. 'I have Scottish ancestry but I've never been there. Where are y'all from?' Before the adults could reply, eight-year-old Bruce leapt in: 'Peebles,' he said proudly. 'P-e-e-b-l-e-s?' said the American, making it sound like Pee-bless. He was now dealing with Bruce as the three adults looked on proudly.

'That's wonderful. And what's your name, sonny?' 'Bruce,' said Bruce. 'Lovely old Scottish name, Bruce. Are you all staying in this nice hotel like we are?' 'Oh yes, it's great here,' said Bruce, jumping up and down excitedly. 'We've got two really, really big rooms.' Then he added, unnecessarily, 'I sleep with my Mum, and Gran sleeps with Dad.' The American suddenly seemed less proud of his Scottish ancestry. 'Oh, really,' he said as they fled.

Texan salmonella

The last talk before the break at a scientific session I attended in Boston was about the safety of marine foods regarding things like bacterial contamination. At the break we trooped out and there were tall stacks of white Styrofoam cups, four massive coffee urns and piles of sugar-glazed doughnuts of an orangey hue. I filled my Styrofoam cup, grabbed a doughnut and moved to the side as the delegates poured out of the lecture hall. A giant behind me with red hair grabbed a coffee and four doughnuts and joined me. 'How-de-do, I'm Dale, from Galveston, Texas. Good talk that last one,' he said, as the first doughnut went down. What with the Styrofoam and the doughnuts we couldn't shake hands which was just as well as I think he would have left my hand with multiple fractures. 'Hello, Dale. Nice to meet you. I'm Malcolm, over from England.'

There was a silence as the second doughnut joined the first so I opened the conversation. 'Yes, it was interesting, Dale. Do you have much of a problem with salmonella in Texan seafood?' He looked at me and nodded but the third doughnut was on its way down. When it was below the line at which he was able to speak he said, 'Gee, Mal, we sure do. Down there in Texas, we got salmonella as big as rats.' It was sinking in that everything is bigger in America.

California: The Film Star (1966)

Bob's mother was coming home so we moved out, but she kindly offered me the Ford Fairlane for $250 and I jumped at the chance. The University of California owned a group of apartments on Sepulveda Boulevard, not far from MGM Studios, and we got one. The apartments were unfurnished but there was a furniture warehouse run by university volunteers. You took what you needed, putting it back when you moved on, together with anything else you had bought. There were tables and chairs, carpets, sofas, pots and pans, TVs, beds etc. We managed to furnish most of the apartment and then Bob's wife, Mary, told me that the famous actor Michael Wilding, Elizabeth Taylor's first husband, had some nice furnishings that he was getting rid of and, being English, would be glad to see it go to a fellow Brit. Mary knew this because she and the Wildings shared a cleaning lady.

Michael Wilding lived not far away, in Beverly Hills, so after calling his housekeeper I drove over there. She didn't seem to know much about it and was vague, but had asked me to come over at noon the next day. My 1957 Ford Fairlane rolled up on its whitewall tyres at the door of a fancy Hollywood mansion. I hadn't expected to see the great film star himself, just what he wanted rid of. Mary told us there were lovely curtains and we didn't have any at that early stage, which meant three-month-old Suzie was waking up as soon as the sun came up. The sun came out daily in California.

I knocked and was admitted to the house. 'Mr Wilding isn't up yet,' said the housekeeper. 'Please wait for him here.' I was shown into a room that, on the face of it, was a nice room; it looked onto the canyons of Beverly Hills and to a private garden with palm trees and flowers. The coffee table was badly damaged – one leg was nearly bent off and the top was cracked. Other furniture showed marks of damage and there were recent bad stains on the carpet. The housekeeper said nothing about the state of the room and left me there for over thirty minutes. I was uncomfortable, awaiting an interview with the famous film star about furnishings, which looked like they might be wrecked anyway.

The curtains looked expensive though and I wondered if they were the ones.

After forty minutes I began to make to go but the housekeeper wasn't there and it would have been rude to just leave. There was a noise of someone trailing down the stairs and a grey-looking man in a dressing gown with the face of someone with a terrible hangover dragged himself into the room. He peered at me and then at the wrecked furniture. 'Had a few friends over last night…. a bit of a party,' he said. I hadn't realised that parties in Hollywood involved wrecking the furniture but I wanted to get out of there. He seemed to be unable to concentrate. I said, 'I just dropped by at the suggestion of Mrs Pecsok. I've arrived here for two years' research at UCLA and we're furnishing an apartment. She said there were items you needed to get rid of.'

He glowered at me through his hangover and held his head. I wished I had never come. 'Yes, well, we might be getting rid of stuff, drapes and some furniture,' he said. I didn't know what that meant as I understood he wanted rid of furnishings and as we were both English it might help. So I said, 'Well, that's fine, I'm sure Mrs Pecsok will let me know when you do.' There was an uncomfortable silence and I sensed that perhaps underneath he wanted to know what I would pay for his drapes and furnishings. I didn't see this conversation going anywhere; this screen heartthrob who had been married to the most beautiful woman and most famous film star in the world was as wrecked as his coffee table. I thanked him and left with a wan smile from the housekeeper.

It was a sad house and I wondered what kind of 'friends' wrecked your house. But I heard no more and we found curtains at the cooperative. Alas, even with the nice curtains I did not stay in California because Margaret became very ill again and was admitted to the psychiatric unit at the teaching hospital at UCLA. We had no family there and the US is no place to be if you have a mental illness – insurances don't cover the long-stay care that this often requires. So, after two years, I started to think of finding a job back home. One found me, a laboratory in Kingston upon Hull, where I switched from intermolecular forces to fisheries, surely a sign of insanity.

Kingston upon Hull: Escape to a new life? (1968)

The British government was worried about the number of science PhDs going to America, the so-called brain drain, and they sent over teams of recruiters to tempt us back. I had five offers and one I fancied was to work on fisheries research at a small laboratory in Hull. It was a long way from intermolecular forces but I was ready to do something different that might be more practically useful; there were only two or three other people in the world that I could talk to about what I was doing on intermolecular forces. So I found myself on a freezing December Sunday night back from California, in a cheap boarding house in Hull on a street called The Boulevard, a misnomer. I was walking out of glorious Technicolor life into a dismal black-and-white one.

Worse, the boarding house was miserably depressing: the carpets were greasy, the bedrooms were tiny with wafer-thin walls and the food was dreadful, none of those lovely steaks and salads I had become used to in Santa Monica. I reported to the laboratory for my first day with foreboding. The weather was miserable, the place bleak. Unlike the friendly egalitarianism of America, the boss was stuffy and Victorian and called me only by my surname. Whatever had I done? I was already homesick for California. The first week the three of us scientists based in the small Humber Laboratory, an outstation, took the sleeper train from York up to the main research station in Aberdeen, where I was to meet my new colleagues.

It was a shock to reach Aberdeen in mid-winter, the city was dark nearly all day and after the shops in California, bursting with fruit and vegetables, all I saw in the greengrocer's shops as we trudged through the icy town were root vegetables carrots, turnips and potatoes. There was a meeting of the staff and I was introduced as the new guy who had just arrived from California, a physical chemist. After the meeting broke up, a lanky, sandy-haired guy with a twisted grin came up to me. 'Malcolm, my name is Roy. I'm a chemist too, it's so nice to have another chemist on the team. Until you came I was the only one here.' It cheered me to think that here, at least, I had an ally.

Roy was friendly. I needed that. I had just given up my job in LA, crossed the Atlantic, was missing California and was 500 miles from my family, my wife was again in a mental hospital and my daughter Suzie was with her grandparents. I was in the first ten days of this new job, which had required major changes to my life. 'Roy,' I said, 'it seems a good lab. I liked the director. The people I have met so far seem nice. You've been here longer, what sort of a place is it and have you any advice for me?' Roy pulled himself out of his chair, walked across to the window and stared out at Aberdeen harbour where fishing boats were coming and going.

'Yes, I have,' he said. I looked up eagerly; this sort of advice from someone who knew the score, knew how things worked, might be helpful to me in starting out on a totally new job in totally new field in a place far from home. But Roy continued to stare out of the window as if he had forgotten my question. I stood up and walked over to him. He turned around and looked me in the eye. 'If I were you I'd get out of here as soon as possible.'

Back in Hull, with Roy's advice ringing in my ears, it was almost Christmas. Hull was still a long way away from Bristol, and I needed wheels – even if they were to be without whitewall tyres. I took the engineer from the laboratory to the address given in the advertisement for the private sale of a Hillman Minx estate car. When we arrived the car was connected to a battery charger but our engineer looked at it and pronounced himself generally satisfied, though since his main stock-in-trade was fish-filleting equipment I am not sure whether he meant that it would fillet a haddock or was the cheap and reliable family car I was searching for.

It was the Monday before Christmas and I was to leave Hull for Bristol on the Friday, Christmas Eve. I bought the car for the asking price. The next morning it would not start and I discovered the reason: the battery was knackered. That was not too serious and I bought a new one. This was my first car in Europe and I cleaned it in preparation for the long journey from Hull to Bristol. There was hardly any motorway then – just a few miles of the M1 – so the drive took seven hours. At around 11 a.m. on Christmas Eve the Victorian boss suggested I might leave; nothing was being done by the staff, who sat there determined not to do any work but not permitted to clear off.

I said my farewells and set off, doing well for the first ninety miles. I just got onto the only patch of motorway when I heard a banging noise from the engine. I thought it might sort itself out if I just eased up a few miles an hour and this is what I did. It did not sort itself out but stayed the same. It was hard for me to accept that my new purchase was defective, or at least that it had become sick so quickly. But it had, and suddenly all sorts of lights lit up on the dashboard, all of them warning of something terrible. I saw that there was an exit ramp in a few hundred yards and decided to coast into it.

But then there was an explosion, very loud indeed, black smoke, swirled like a small tornado across the motorway from the engine compartment and then I was without power at all. By luck it was downhill into the service station and I pulled up in a cloud of smoke, hot oil pouring from the engine, outside the AA kiosk. The attendant came out to see what the noise and smoke was all about. He shook his head gravely as the smoke cleared and he opened the bonnet. There was, I now saw, a hole in the side of the engine. A connecting rod, so he told me, had come apart with such force that it had smashed through the engine casing.

'I'm heading home for Christmas,' I said, and added weakly and as it turned out rather stupidly, 'can you patch it up temporarily?' He replied that not only could he not do that but also that it needed a completely new engine, which would take weeks. He asked where I was heading. It was now past four o'clock on Christmas Eve and I was still 160 miles from home. I should, in his opinion, get myself to the nearest railway station as soon as possible if I did not want to spend Christmas on a motorway verge. I should leave the car with him and arrange to have it collected and a new engine fitted.

He moved on to the next worried customer, a young lady with a problem with her Austin Mini. Quite apart from finding a taxi at a motorway service station, I had no idea where the nearest railway station might be where there were trains to Bristol. As the young lady waited for the mechanic to fix her car – it turned out to require just an adjustment to the carburettor – I plucked up the courage to begin a conversation. 'I'm in a bit of a mess,' I said. 'My car has blown a hole in its engine.' She made sympathetic noises. 'Do you happen to be going south or west? I would really appreciate a lift part of the way, I'm heading for Bristol.'

She gave me a hard look up and down. She was nice, attractive, bookish, with golden blonde hair and wearing a full-skirted red dress. The car back seat was full of presents. There was a pause, and then she said, 'I'm going to Oxford and I'm happy to take you there. I think there are trains to Bristol from Oxford.' I moved my case from the still gently smoking Hillman into the boot of the Mini, told the AA man I'd arrange to have the car collected and we set off, two strangers on Christmas Eve with different plans for Christmas. She drove slowly and nervously; I offered to drive but she didn't accept. We began to chat and the atmosphere quickened. She didn't seem to regret picking me up; in fact, she started to converse more and more animatedly.

I told her I had only been in Hull for three weeks and had recently returned from two years at the University of California. She was embarking on a university career in Leeds as a junior lecturer and had just finished her first term. She was returning to her parents in Oxford for Christmas. She was an only child and, from the way she spoke of him, close to her father. It grew dark and in the glow of the lights we spoke in an easy way. She laughed at my stories of life in California. She knew I was also going to spend Christmas with my parents but asked no more about my situation.

Our conversation flowed as if we were old friends. I wondered what time we might get to Oxford at the speed she was driving, not before seven or eight at night I thought. Was there a train to Bristol so late on Christmas Eve? As we neared the city she said that rather than drive in to the station she wanted to take me home and let her father phone the station – she wanted me to meet her parents and no doubt I was hungry. She was taking a shine to me.

I suddenly realised I had not said anything about the fact that I was married, that my wife was sick and in a mental hospital and that I had a two-year-old daughter. Since I was travelling alone, going home to my parents for Christmas, she had reasonably assumed that I was single, though she hadn't asked. She was so easy to talk to and I realised what I was missing in my marriage to a schizophrenic lady who was lovely but where communication tended to become crippled by the vagaries of the illness and the delusions that she suffered. I protested mildly that it would inconvenience her and her parents to have me, a total stranger, dropping in late on Christmas Eve. But she insisted; the station was in any case across the other side of Oxford and it might be that there were no trains to Bristol until the day after Boxing Day.

I sensed she wished this was so and I too began to picture a different Christmas without the curse that is schizophrenia. As we reached the lights of Oxford I felt a growing temptation to start another life with a new identity, to escape my present predicament and just disappear. The perfect opportunity had fallen into my lap. We arrived at her house; it was beautifully decorated for Christmas, a log fire was burning, and the much-loved daughter was returning home. She introduced me to her parents, so different to my own parents-in-law.

She told them animatedly how we had met and that we had spent the last four hours in the car together. They were civilised, welcoming and I was aware that they had picked up vibes. Something had happened. They saw it at once in her demeanour. Charlotte, their only child, had found a man on Christmas Eve by pure chance and she was already keen. Perhaps they were concerned that she was in her late twenties at a time when most girls were married before the age of twenty-five. She was clearly very keen for them to like me. I did like them; they made me welcome and Charlotte's father poured me my first gin and tonic since I had left California.

I apologised for my arrival but they would have nothing of it. Charlotte and her mother disappeared for a short time and there was an urgent conversation in the kitchen between them, which I could not hear, while I chatted to Daddy by the log fire, downing my powerful G&T. We liked one another too. Mother and daughter suddenly returned to the drawing room, seemingly itching to announce something. 'Malcolm, we doubt you will be able to get to Bristol tonight. Even if you can it will be a terrible journey. You are most welcome to stay a night or so until the trains run again. We have plenty of room. Please do.' Potential new father-in-law nodded vigorously. I must have hesitated; I said it was terrifically kind but my parents would worry.

Of course they easily countered that by inviting me to phone them and explain. Charlotte looked at me in an intense way and now I saw her properly she was more animated and attractive. A wave of emotion swept over me; I was still in my twenties, just, and this could be another existence with no sick wife, no dreadful in-laws. Maybe I too could return to academic life and get a position in Oxford or even go back to California. Even my new colleague, Roy, had advised me to get away, though I had just arrived.

I wanted desperately to say, 'Yes, yes, let's do that, no need to phone my folks.' It would make a lovely carefree Christmas compared to the Christmas that I was facing, one of harrowing visits to a Victorian mental hospital every day followed by a return to the miserable boarding house in Hull (without a car). They must have sensed that I was in a kind of dilemma. Charlotte and her mother, even her father, all three looked at me as if saying, 'Please say yes.' I badly, badly wanted to say yes but I knew I was drifting into a fantasy land. I couldn't do it. If it hadn't been for my two-year-old daughter, Suzie, maybe I would have.

I said that if there was a train, I had to take it but I did not give a reason; somehow it would have broken the lovely spell if I revealed the complexity of everything. As I stood there, close to Charlotte, not wanting this to end, her Father phoned the station; the last train was in thirty-five minutes and got me into Bristol at 1 a.m. He drove me to the station. I was sad for the Christmas and the new life that might have been. But at least I had my lovely two-year-old for Christmas, who was happy with her grandparents and fortunately knew as little about the situation I was in as did Charlotte.

Amsterdam: Red light (but not the district) (1969)

It was an international fisheries meeting. Margaret had recovered and was within a few days of giving birth to our second child, Sarah. It was long before the days of mobile phones but I had given her the number of the Amsterdam hotel, which was newly built. So, of course, I was anxious to know when there were any messages for me. I asked the receptionist. 'Yes, sir, we have a message indicator in every room. It's a brand-new system and if there is a message for you the red light on the edge of your bedside table will come on and stay on until you have received the message.

'Excellent. I took the lift to my room and showered after the journey. When I got back into the bedroom the red message light was on. Had my wife given birth in the last four minutes? I phoned reception breathlessly. 'My red message light is on. Is there a message for me?' 'No, sir, no messages.' 'Well, my red light is on.' 'I don't understand that, sir. I will get the technician to investigate.' Over the next few days, every time I came back to the hotel the red light was on and every time I phoned the reception I was told that there was no message and the technician would investigate. The red light burned all night so I put a sock over it just to get to sleep, but I was never sure that there wasn't a real message. On my last evening before flying home I came back into the room and the red light was off. This was a major change, the first time in four days that it had gone off.

I phoned reception. 'My red light has been on for four days, now it is off.' 'Yes,' she said, 'there is a message here for you from your wife.' 'What is it?' 'She left a message to say she hasn't had the baby.'

Hull/London: The men from the Ministry (1969)

Have you ever been to a meeting which you thought afterwards that you were mad to have gone to and wondered why on earth it had been called in the first place? I expect you have. I have been to lots in the British Civil Service. I was at many meetings that were expected to achieve nothing, to ensure that nothing new happened, and mainly to show that there had been 'a meeting'. But this one I was responsible for – it was my fault. As a researcher newly returned from America I asked my boss at the Humber fisheries research station in Hull what the government policy was on industrial fishing.

I wanted to know because the industry was pressing me to do more research on the uses of and processing of industrial fish. These are species such as sprats and sand eels that are rich in proteins and oils but are not consumed by humans directly because they are small, bony and oily. But they are consumed in large tonnages through animal feed. We were and are eating them in the form of chicken, pork and farmed salmon. In fact, more fish is eaten indirectly through feeding to other animals than is eaten directly. It was not a minor issue.

My question was whether the government wanted to encourage industrial fishery as a way of utilising our large marine resources and to make us more self-sufficient in animal feed, or to discourage it because it might take the food of the fish that we do eat and might affect bird populations? My Victorian boss suggested I write to the Fisheries Secretary at the ministry in London and ask that question. There was little point in devoting our scarce fisheries research resources to an area where the government was negative. On the other hand, there was a good opportunity to develop under-utilised stocks to produce a primary product that we imported in large amounts, adding to the current balance of payment problems.

Moreover, the Danes were busy exploiting it and by feeding the non-food fish, in the form of fishmeal, to pigs and chickens developed a prosperous Danish pork, bacon and poultry industry. The fish stocks being used were ours and what we were doing was letting the Danes use our marine resources and then importing our own fish back in the form of Danish bacon. The Fisheries Secretary's letter of reply arrived quickly, saying that I should come to a meeting in London three weeks hence at 3 p.m., no other comment. I had no idea whether the meeting would have been held anyway or whether it was only being held because of my letter, who might be there and what angle on industrial fishing was to be discussed.

But I was impressed – the British system was working. I would go to London, they would tell me what the policy was and I would tailor my research programme to fit that policy. The department would not waste money on unnecessary research and the industry that had asked the question would learn of the ministry's attitude to their initiative. Public funds would be used in a way that was tuned to public policy and industry needs. It would be democracy in action – or so I thought.

I rose with the East Yorkshire dawn, took a taxi smelling faintly of haddock to the station and travelled to London, where I bought a sandwich in a pub near the ministry. I was nervous; I had heard about top civil servants, that they were bright, Oxbridge educated and sophisticated in their use of language, often using Latin phrases. I had not been in the headquarters of the Ministry of Agriculture, Fisheries and Food before. It was imposing, with lions on the pillars outside. I was carefully scrutinised and taken upstairs through hushed corridors until we reached a large doorway.

Inside, a thickset woman with tightly permed hair, wearing a grey cardigan and smelling of cigarettes, took my coat and told me that the Secretary was in a meeting which would end shortly. She offered me disgustingly strong, sweet tea. They seemed to have their own tea fiefdom because on the way up I saw a notice stuck on a noticeboard that private kettles were not allowed. Hot water should be obtained from the Urn Room it said. I pictured the Urn Room as holding the ashes of Permanent Secretaries Past. But her boss must have been so senior that she could get a dispensation from the Kettle Rule. Was there a Kettles Sub-Committee?

I sipped the strong, sweet tea and just about heard the drone of measured voices from within. I wondered whether this was a meeting on some other subject or preparation for the meeting that I was here for. After not too long the door was opened and a man with pebble glasses came out. 'Dr Windsor,' he said, 'do come in.' I was shown into a room that already held five people. He introduced them; they were all called Secretaries of one kind or another. I sat down in the only place available, at the other end of the table from the Fisheries Secretary who was at the rank of Deputy Secretary. The other staff looked at me without much curiosity but with a slight interest. I came from a port that, though central to fishing and to everything that made their job necessary, they had almost certainly never been to.

The Fisheries Secretary peered at me through his extraordinarily thick glasses; I wondered how he read all the papers that were supposed to cross the desks of top civil servants each day. He seemed detached but cautious and well mannered. His striped shirt did not seem to be the cleanest, as if he had worn it through the London air for more than a day. His suit similarly a little stale, if good quality. He began the meeting as if I was being interviewed. 'Thank you so much, Dr Windsor, from coming down from Grimsby today.' He doesn't know the difference 'tween Grimsby and Hull, I thought – a hanging offence in the East Riding.

'Perhaps we can start right away on this matter before us.' The previous meeting between them must have been a preparation to resolve the issues before my arrival. I was impressed. They were going to tell me, no doubt in immaculate English and a phrase or two in Latin, their policy towards industrial fishing. He turned to the Assistant Secretary who he described as overseeing ports, fisheries and research. He asked him to introduce the subject. The Assistant Secretary, in an equally measured way, started into an introduction of the subject. I soon realised that this was not a man who called a spade a spade.

'Well, Mr Secretary,' he said. 'Cognisant of the request from the Humber Laboratory I can say that, bearing in mind the present situation vis-à-vis the European Commission and having regard to the internal policy needs of the ministry, I believe that it may be untimely and perhaps even unwise to proceed with an alliteration of policy needs at this particular juncture.' He paused and took a breath, the others nodded gravely. 'Nevertheless, and we have had representations from certain quarters of which you will be aware, Division 2c's opinion is that it is premature to embark on specific programmes at this stage. That is not to say that preliminary and useful discussions should not proceed even now to deal with some of the outline issues.'

He rambled on in this vein for at least fifteen minutes, in a jargon now recognisable as being straight out of the TV programme Yes Minister but the first episode of that was not transmitted for another nine years. I didn't know the code then and didn't have a clue what he was proposing. He then suggested setting up some sort of committee, which might meet at an unspecified future date to, as he put it, clarify the issues involved. He said that due to the pressure of other matters and the heavy workload of Division 2c, he did not foresee such a group being assembled before the autumn. It was now March.

The Assistant Secretary then asked his Principal, a portly, younger man with a poshed-up South London accent to comment on recent meetings held with the environment ministry. He had obviously studied the form. He spoke in the same style as his superiors but used fewer Latin phrases, if any, and was less sure of himself. The Fisheries Secretary and the Assistant Secretary exchanged a glance while he was speaking that was between a nod and a slight wince. I couldn't tell why. The Principal made more sense to me than the others.

Then I was invited to contribute but it must have been clear to them that I did not understand what they had been saying. I said that I simply wanted to know was whether the government wished to encourage the growth of industrial fishing so that the UK could be more self-sufficient in marine-based animal feedstuffs, or if they wanted to discourage it. I needed to know so as to focus my research programme properly to get the most benefit to the trade balance of the country. At this there was a resounding silence, almost a shock. I wondered what I had said that caused this.

The Secretary with the pebble glasses picked up one of the papers on his desk and held it two inches from his eyes and then gently lowered it onto the table. He sighed. The Assistant Secretary and the Principal looked interested in the ceiling. It was as if I had said something very, very embarrassing. I heard Big Ben strike five o'clock. It seemed to take ages. The Fisheries Secretary came to life again. He beamed benignly at me through the thick glass. 'Well, time is getting on. Most useful,' he said. 'Thank you very much for coming down from Grimsby today. Goodbye.'

I started to form a sentence: 'When will I get an answer to my question?' But it was over, they were tapping their papers together and standing up. My question was not answered, but the ministry had achieved its objective on this issue. There had been 'a meeting' and it had decided to set up a committee at a future date, which never came. It was best not to have a policy on things – then you couldn't go wrong.

Poland: Communist butchery (1973)

Hitler was long gone but other countries were going mad due to the spread of communism led by other despotic leaders, notably Stalin, who was also dead but his empire lived on. Poland was one of the countries that suffered greatly from this, as did most of Eastern Europe. Poland was effectively still occupied by the USSR still under the mad communist regime imposed on it.

Arriving in Warsaw ahead of meeting with a Polish fisheries scientist in Gdansk was depressing; Warsaw looked sad. The hotel was standard communist style: cracked lino, thin curtains, red-hot radiator, hard narrow bed, no bath plug, no TV and a radio only tuneable to the official party radio station. It was a miserable arrival anyway for two reasons: first, I had a nasty attack of haemorrhoids, and second, it was my birthday, spent alone in this dismal Soviet hotel.

I was certain that I was being followed. In reception there was a man who was pretending to read a newspaper and whenever I came in and out he was looking around his newspaper and ready to tail me. True, I was working for the British government and my visit was to a leading marine scientist at our request. My miserable birthday was spent alone in Warsaw and the next day I took the train to Gdansk, where the scientist worked. There I checked into another hotel, which was similar if not worse.

At breakfast next morning I entered the huge dining room, which was empty. No one was there to greet me or seat me so I just I sat down

62

near the door. After ten minutes a waiter came out from the kitchen. He did not seem pleased to see me. In fact, he asked me to move to another table where another waiter was in charge. That waiter came out and in turn asked me to move to a third table as he said his area of the restaurant was closed. I was getting further and further away and each waiter was trying to pass me on to another. Eventually I was served a dismal breakfast and the scientist I was to meet picked me up and we drove to the laboratory.

We discussed research items all day and he was doing good work which was of interest to us. We agreed to cooperate and he was keen. At 4 p.m. as we were finishing for the day he invited me for dinner at a restaurant. 'Thank you very much, that would be nice. What time?' I asked. 'Now,' he said. 'All the restaurants close at 5:30 p.m.' When we got there, at 4:15 p.m., I saw that the restaurant had no name, only a sign outside that read 'Restaurant No. 23'. I discovered that none of the restaurants had names, just numbers. They were all run by the state so the workers closed the restaurants at 5:30 p.m. I was back in the hotel early, just me and my haemorrhoids.

We worked again the next day and this time the scientist invited me to his home for dinner. He gave me directions; it was not far from the hotel but it was a shock to find him in a poorly built tower block in a group of seven or eight blocks, all identical. He was a senior scientist but his apartment was tiny, one bedroom and they had a small boy who slept there so the scientist and his wife slept on the sitting room sofa. But they were marvellously kind and hospitable with food. I was concerned they might have used all the week's food ration just at dinner that night. I tried to ask them how life was but, understandably, it was too risky for them to talk to a foreigner and say anything critical of the regime.

But we laughed and I began to appreciate the Polish humour that allowed them to cope with the dismal regime that they lived under. Before he took me back to the station to get the train to Warsaw he showed me around the central square in Gdansk, which must have been charming once but was now rundown. At one shop there was a huge queue. He showed interest in this and asked a lady at the end of the queue what was she queuing for. 'I don't know,' she said. 'There's a rumour that something is coming in today but I don't know what.' There, outdoors, where we talked without being overheard, he subtly answered my questions of the night before.

In the main square he stopped at an old-fashioned shop with a painted sign in Polish. 'This is how things are under our system,' he said. 'See this shop? Well, before communism the sign outside used to say "butcher" and inside there was just meat. But now, under communism it's the same shop but things are different. They repainted the sign and now outside it says "meat" and inside… there's just a butcher.'

Peru: A malodorous hotel (1974)

Hull was a nicer place to live than I had expected and I also started to be sent abroad more often to attend scientific meetings. An international scientific fisheries meeting was to be held in Lima. Peru took the biggest catch of marine fish in the world, albeit mostly of anchovies. This stock had a curious history of utilisation. Exploitation started off not by harvesting the fish themselves, nor by harvesting the seabirds that feasted on the enormous anchovy stocks. What was harvested was the seabird-produced guano covering the rocks and islets on the Pacific coast of Peru in massive quantities. It was dug up and shipped to Europe as a fertiliser, which was used to grow animal food that was then fed to chickens and pigs.

What a food chain that was. We estimated that it might take at least 1000 kilos of anchovy to produce a kilo of pork or chicken. Things had improved massively since the invention of fishmeal, which cut out the guano/seabird stage and directly rendered the anchovies down to a high protein powder and a rich fish oil that was still sent to Europe but then fed directly to the livestock. A much less wasteful food chain. But there was, at the time, starvation in many parts of the world, particularly in Africa. Could we develop a product from Peruvian anchoveta (a small, bony, oily fish not too attractive to eat as is) that was a concentrated protein, easily shipped, needing no refrigeration and being palatable to those who badly needed the highly nutritional benefits of the product?

That was one of the reasons to go to Lima to meet with other international scientists. South America was new to me and to my delight I was advised that travel was organised for a small group of six of us scientists from Europe and that the most economical way to get there (planes did not have the range they do today) was to fly to Antigua by British Airways, then fly on to Lima by a South American airline, stopping briefly in Ecuador. And it got even better: we had to wait three nights in the Caribbean to make the connection. Terrible nuisance.

While there I swam in the Caribbean Sea for the first time and saw the beautiful corals just off the coast when we snorkelled. By accident

64

my flipper broke off a piece of coral that looked like a bonsai tree, and rather than leave it there I brought it ashore and took it to my room. My daughters had never seen coral and although I felt bad about breaking it off it didn't seem to make things any worse by taking it home to show them how beautiful it was. I wrapped it in lots of toilet paper and put it in my case. That night I felt sharp pains in my fingers and hand and realised that the coral had stinging power. But I guessed this would disappear, as the beautiful coral was now dead in my suitcase.

We travelled on to Peru and were warmly received by government representatives and taken directly to a limousine without going through immigration or customs. It was a military regime, Peru was run by its generals, and I realised later that even holding this international meeting gave the regime some implicit international recognition, which it was lacking. There was growing domestic resistance to the regime, with violent attacks by rebels and even more violent repression by the generals. We were taken to an expensive hotel and told that there was a dinner in our honour at the military academy that night.

An armed convoy took us across the city, past the slums, and when we arrived it was already dark. No social gathering started in Peru until at least 10 p.m. It was warm and dozens of tables were laid outside on a floodlit parade ground, with trees, flowers and shrubs placed among the tables to make it look less military. A military band played and the generals in dress uniform and their elegant ladies were awaiting us. They were warm hosts, no doubt lapping up the legitimacy that they thought the presence of these foreigners was bringing to them. Waiters with slicked-down black hair and chalk-white uniforms circulated with pisco sours. The food was excellent, the wine flowed and the band switched from marches to sambas and cha-cha-chá.

The generals were all short, wearing highly polished black shoes, and their wives were all plump with black hair, high heels and deep crimson lipstick. They were jolly and up for a great night out, thanks to our visit giving them the excuse to use public funds for it. They soon took to the floor with great enthusiasm – they clearly adored to dance. But I didn't have a wife with me and I couldn't dance anyway so I sat gazing at this odd scene of dancing generals. How had I come to be here at a military dinner dance as a prized guest of a repressive Latin American regime but aiming to help feed the starving millions in Africa?

As my gaze wandered to the edges of the dinner tables and past the dance floor, beyond the lights I saw metallic glinting. Peering closer I made out that we were surrounded by a steel ring of armed soldiers.

65

They were silent and almost invisible. The silence did not last too long: there was a crackling noise from 100 metres away followed by shouted commands and a rush of soldiers away from the steel ring, followed by machine-gun fire. I was scared, I thought I should get under the table – we were being fired upon by rebels. I stood up, expecting to be evacuated from this vulnerable place. But the generals and their ladies took absolutely no notice and continued with the samba.

Occasional gunfire continued from the undergrowth beyond the parade ground but it seemed to get further away. The dancing continued until beyond 3 a.m. when we were taken back to the hotel with an even bigger armed convoy. When I walked into the hotel at nearly 4 a.m. there was an odd aroma. In fact, one irate American man in his dressing gown was at the front desk saying he must move rooms because his room on the eighth floor had an awful smell. The receptionist was apologising profusely and, as I waited for my key, I heard her say she would send a porter to move him at once. I was on the ninth floor and the smell was on my floor too. It was curious because it was faint, not overpowering, but sickly and a little nauseating.

The next day at breakfast the smell was still there but not strong, at least in the dining room. I left the hotel to go to the first day of the scientific conference. A general, showing no signs of damage from the all-night samba-ing, welcomed us formally. At each place in the conference room were several gifts, pens and key rings, which looked expensive but fell apart almost as soon as you put them in your pocket. The general left and we set about our work; the day went well and we made progress on the ideas to develop the fish protein concentrate that might save the 'starving millions'. I returned to the hotel and as I picked up my key there were a few people asking to change rooms and some were even checking out.

They seemed angry and there was more talk of the smell. And I smelt it. On the ninth floor the malodour was still evident and it was in my room too, but no worse in my room than in the corridors – even the lifts smelt. Though unpleasant, it was still faint, and I think I might have checked out myself except that we were on a group booking and staying for three more days. At least we were out all day at the conference. When I turned off the light to sleep it got worse; as my other senses closed down the sense of smell heightened. I got to sleep only by keeping my head under the sheet until, half suffocating, I dozed off.

During the night there was an earthquake. It woke me as the building swayed, I imagined more on the ninth floor than below. I heard sharp cracks as some of the bathroom tiles fell off the wall and into the

66

bath. Perhaps, I dreamt, the smell was a sign of an impending earthquake as vapours arose from inside the earth. Next morning, I stopped at reception to tell them about the bathroom damage. They said there were many earthquakes in Lima, it happened a lot, and they would replace the tiles while I was out. I mentioned the smell and my new theory. They dismissed it brusquely, they said there were many earthquakes but none of them had made a smell before. They were mystified as to the origin of the bad odour. They had searched everywhere but not found any source in the whole hotel.

There was no point in moving me because it was everywhere, in every corridor, in every restaurant, in every bedroom. The manager happened to be there and apologised. He appeared to be on the edge of a nervous breakdown, over the last few days half of the guests had checked out to find another hotel because of the smell, even though this was the best hotel in the capital. The military government had been contacted but no one had experienced anything like it. The next night when I got back to the hotel it was even worse: what had been faint, cloying and sickly was now stronger and more nauseating.

It was the same in my room. I was glad we were going out to eat. I grabbed my suitcase for the first time since arriving to get a smart shirt, as the Peruvians dressed up to go out. When I opened the suitcase it was as if I had disinterred a festering carcass. A cloud of nauseating vapour emerged. It was the coral. It was now dead and the hundreds of micro-organisms that make up coral were rotting away in different ways and at different speeds to produce a cocktail of horrible stinks that possessed the ability to permeate into every room on every floor of the best hotel in Peru. The terrible realisation came to me that I, or my coral sample, was the source of this misery, upheaval and economic damage to the business of this splendid hotel.

I had to get it out of the hotel without alerting anyone to the fact that I was the culprit. I grabbed a plastic laundry bag and put the festering coral into one, then wrapped it in another one, then another, until I used up every single laundry bag in the room. I put the bag over my arm and draped a coat over the bag. I descended to the reception, where I saw more people checking out. Some were checking out even before they had checked in. The miasma of coral death filled the air. I walked hastily out into the main square, my coat covering the multiple laundry bags.

I walked at least a mile, frequently looking over my shoulder as I passed peasant ladies with bowler hats selling vegetables and fruit. They saw I was a foreigner and were misguidedly trying to attract my attention. They didn't know how lucky they were that I rushed onwards, refusing their invitations to stop at their stalls. Their produce would have been unsaleable if I had even paused for a moment near their food. I was terribly scared too that the odour was so strong that the military could easily follow my trail, even without any sniffer dogs, and if they found me I would be going back to the same barracks, not to a dance but as a prisoner charged with serious economic damage to Peru.

After a mile or so I found myself in a quieter area of the city centre and miraculously, because there were few, I found a litter bin. I skulked around until I was sure no one saw me, lifted the coat on my arm and pushed the six laundry bags with their small cargo into the bin. I turned back as if I had suddenly decided to do a U-turn.

I returned to the hotel by a different route and wondered if I smelt nauseating myself from being in such close contact with the source. But when I entered the hotel the smell had lessened. Or was it that my scent organs were so suffused with it that it was impossible to tell? Perhaps, the removal of the source accomplished, it was already fading away. Back in my room the smell was less but my clean clothes in the suitcase smelt terrible. I had to get them laundered but now I didn't have any laundry bags.

We did develop test production of the fish protein concentrate. It was taken to South Africa as a trial to improve the nutrition of vulnerable populations. The reports came back on the trial: 'Even people who were starving would not eat it.'

London: Lord Rothschild's Remedy (1975)

Yuri Gagarin was unfortunately now dead; after he returned a hero from space he crashed his airplane (some claimed he was drunk at the controls). He couldn't help me anymore, but Mrs Thatcher did. She had been a research chemist herself and she was appointed as Secretary of State for Education and Science. It bothered her that huge expenditures were being made in government-funded science without a clear idea of what it was for. The directors of the many government research institutes did more or less as they wished. Mrs T wanted to know what were the objectives and was the taxpayer getting value for money?

The government asked Lord Rothschild to come up with answers. He concluded that, 'However distinguished, intelligent and practical scientists may be, they cannot decide what the needs of the nation are and their priorities, as those responsible for ensuring those needs are met.' He recommended that there should be a customer/contractor relationship where an independent body, led by scientists in London, decided whether or not to sign the cheques for the research. The Ministry of Agriculture, Fisheries and Food (MAFF), as all the other Ministries doing research, were ordered to adopt this principle, and so a Chief Scientists' Group was set up.

So thanks to Maggie I left the laboratory in Hull and joined the Chief Scientists' Group as the man who dealt with marine research. I was to advise which research had a customer need to be funded by the taxpayer and which did not. Sir Charles Pereira was the Chief Scientist he was an agricultural scientist and had spent years in Africa. He was a short, agile, dapper man with nice suits and sleek hair swept straight back and curled up at his neck. He had a certain charm. If you saw him, you might have guessed that he was a tango dancer in an Argentine salon – and his footwork was fancy. He talked so much at such length that I wondered how he even took any information in, yet he did seem to. He listened for odd details and trotted them out on visits to laboratories, astonishing the scientists.

He had the knack that some – not me – seem to have of arriving exactly on time for everything, not a second too early, not a second too late. Once, we were going to the end of the world together – well to Burnham-on-Crouch in Essex – where MAFF had a small laboratory. We arranged to meet at Liverpool Street Station to catch the 8.35 a.m. train. Just as it was pulling out Sir Charles pranced in from the shadows; he neatly opened a carriage door near mine and sailed in, not in the least ruffled. 'Good morning,' he said. 'What are we going to see today?'

I told him about the work they were doing and which parts of it I believed were well worth doing and which weren't. He didn't seem to take much of this in and talked of other things, mainly Africa. When we arrived the red carpet was out and we were given the treatment, going from the director to one scientist, then another and another. Sir Charles appeared to listen attentively and then would ask a question of such detail that the scientists were astonished. One scientist was telling us of his work of monitoring pollution levels of heavy metals and pesticides in the North Sea by regularly sampling molluscs, which concentrated the metals cadmium, zinc and lead. He did a complex chemical analysis to determine the levels and how they varied over time. In the middle of this long explanation Sir Charles would suddenly say, 'Ah yes, analysis for zinc – what it the pH you use for that titration, about nine?'

Of course the fellow was amazed that Sir Charles had such a grasp not only of the grand scheme of things in the whole of the national

R&D programmes, and not only in the monitoring of the heavy metals in molluscs in the North Sea, but in the minute detail of the conditions under which one analysed for zinc. It was bluff; he cleverly picked up the odd detail from here and there and threw it back in to impress. And impress it did. Afterwards they said to me, 'My God, your boss has an amazing grasp of things.' I smiled, picking up kudos from the fact that he appeared to have been so well briefed. Though of course I hadn't told him these things because I didn't know them.

My direct boss was the Deputy Chief Scientist, George Elton, who had worked in the food industry and whose claim to fame there was that he invented the Chorleywood Continuous Bread Making Process. This had been the technology that brought in the dreadful Wonderloaf. It was a wonder you could eat it. George had a wry sense of humour. He told me his first job when leaving school like me at sixteen was with a coal merchant who operated from railway sidings at Wimbledon station. With coal being sold by the hundredweight sack, George's first job was to water the coal and the sacks so it weighed more. How the Wimbledon householders managed to light the fuel that George spent all day watering in the early 1950s he did not know. But the coal merchant grew rich selling water at the price of coal and George, having learnt the physical properties of H2O, moved on to a career in science.

I got the impression that he was serious about changing the structure of £25 million of marine research, involving hundreds of scientists and support staff, six or eight research vessels and tens of millions of pounds' worth of buildings and equipment. We worked in a ghastly office block in Horseferry Road called Great Westminster House. The tawdry corridors led to mean, stuffy rooms with corroding metal windows looking out on council flats. In a desperate attempt to make the building, with its infinite lines of corridors, less tedious, someone at the Property Services Agency had decreed that each door should be painted a different colour, up to a maximum of eight (previously authorised) colours. As you traversed the bureaucratic maze you passed a bright yellow hardboard door followed by purple, lime green, pink, grey, orange, blue and black.

I was given a purple-doored room plus a secretary, Maria. Maria was married to a man from Brixton but was herself of Sicilian origin. Her English was poor and highly accented and her typing was terrible but she used to kiss me hello every morning. She was certainly racist, didn't seem to like black people much, she often told me that 'they ought to be repatronised'.

70

A cosy relationship existed between the administrators in London and the fisheries laboratories. The administrators asked for any scientific advice they wanted from the labs and received it promptly. In return the administrators let the directors of the laboratories get on and do whatever they liked, almost as if they were university departments. Of course, there was a budget but administrators never questioned the programmes themselves. Our remit was to end that cosiness; this meant that both the administrators and the scientific directors had something to lose. At our first meeting George and I met just with the administrators.

It was a hostile reception. We talked about the new Rothschild policy, which, after all, the democratically elected government of the United Kingdom had decided to apply. But the top civil servants saw this new policy as an affront; it suggested a criticism of past practices, which they found impossible to accept. It brought scientists into headquarters, which the administrators didn't like at all. Scientist were not meant to be on top, they were on tap. The clear message I got was that they realised the reasons I had been appointed, they knew the Rothschild customer-contractor principle had to be applied to all government research, but they made it clear, in the subtlest possible way – with a bit of Latin thrown in – that I should, so to speak, pretend do it without changing anything since the whole thing worked well the way it was.

I, taken aback, suggested that I had not moved from Yorkshire to London just to pretend to do a job, which, in any case, I believed was necessary. This did not go down well: the battle lines were being drawn up even as we left. George didn't react to this at the meeting but when we got back to his office he talked as if he was unconcerned and we would fight to implement the changes. He was a bit too nice to take on these senior civil servants protecting their turf. He and I prepared for our battles and he always encouraged me to go out with guns blazing, but when the other side fought back we usually lost. They made the rules and had the ammunition and big departments to protect. We were a few scientists marooned in HQ with little backing. I began to believe that it was a nice cosy plot.

The top brass at MAFF didn't want a thing to change and the customer-contractor principle might not last after the next election, and they would still be there. I struggled against a strong tide and found myself sinking. Later, Sir Charles took a holiday and while he was away the edict from the Cabinet Office came that there was to a be a cut in the most senior staff at the ministry. When he came back from holiday the others at that level, all non-scientists, told him that one post

71

at their level had to go and that while he was away they had decided it was him. The influence of a scientist at the top was lost or downgraded. The jungle was reclaiming its own and the rejection mechanisms by which a bureaucracy always resists change were beavering away to get back to the status quo.

I was more and more frustrated: much needed to be done, money was being wasted and work duplicated, and a proportion of the work was not necessary at all from the public purse. But I was stuck in the maze. Here was craziness: the government of the day decided to adopt a new policy to get better value for money for the taxpayer. Their employees, the civil servants, didn't like the change because it implied that the way it was done before was wrong and that was an impossible thought.

Lowestoft: The west winds do blow (1976)

We moved down to London to a house in Surrey that had been unoccupied for a year or so. It was to be one of the warmest summers for decades and the day that we moved from Yorkshire the weather became very hot indeed. Suzie was now ten years old and Sarah was seven years old and soon Sarah and I were both out in the large garden. It was a jungle, waist high even to me, with tangled dried grass and shrubs. I bought a machete to cut it down so we might have a lawn like the other houses. Sarah wanted to help me but it was over her head as we toiled in the searing heat. She suddenly stopped and waded through the undergrowth to me. She seemed upset, and I put down the machete. 'Dad, Dad! You know I had all that money in the building society.' She was proud that she had £12.50 in the Britannia building society in Hull. 'Well, I left it in England.' I reassured her that we were still in England.

I was away much of the time travelling the coastline of the country to labs large and small; Aberdeen, Pitlochry, Conway, Plymouth, Hull and Lowestoft. At each institute or university, I went to the team leader and asked the same questions. What are you doing? Why are you doing it? Why should the taxpayer be funding it? What would happen if you didn't do it? You can guess that they were not pleased to see me.

This last question often produced a baffled response. It varied from the lucid to the totally incomprehensible. One distinguished scientist, Roy, was completely hidden by piles of books, which I peered over to speak to him when I was shown into his office. I spent hours with him and finally grasped that he was studying the migration of plaice. This needed two research vessels at £15,000 per day plus their crews, ten scientific staff and sophisticated radio tags that were inserted into the plaice unfortunate enough to be chosen to participate in the experiment. The two vessels using radio tracking devices followed the plaice for days on end, measuring their speed, their depth, the time when and where they stopped and the wind speed and current.

All this data took months to analyse and scientific papers were prepared, refereed and published after years of work. It showed, he said, that there was an interesting movement of the plaice stocks in the North Sea. During conditions of the prevailing west wind the plaice stocks tended to migrate to the seabed. There were diurnal vertical migrations, which he showed were linked to daylight length. Roy made a name for himself with this work; he was lively, enthusiastic, eccentric and would have been an excellent university teacher.

One evening in the town I had a drink with a fisherman I knew. The local fishermen used to call the fisheries laboratory 'the University' and they always claimed that nothing ever came out of it of any use to them. To be fair, the work was designed to be of use to the ministry rather than to industry. He asked me how I had passed the day and I told him enthusiastically about the migration of the plaice the results of Roy's ground-breaking ten-year research programme that uncovered how the plaice move. He listened to my summary of Roy's ten years of work, and then he laughed.

'The fishermen have known that for hundreds of years, there's a common saying: 'When the west wind do blow, the plaice do lay low. At night and sunrise, the plaice all do rise.'

It encapsulated in four lines everything Roy had told me. If only Roy had spoken first to the fishermen in the town where he worked, the taxpayer might have saved tens of thousands of pounds. But then there was no dialogue between the fishermen and the fisheries scientists. Now there is.

France: The wheel bearings (1978)

I had been in the job for three years and the summer holidays were coming up, a great feeling. It was Friday and we were off to the Dordogne, where we had never been. Things had greatly changed domestically too. Poor Margaret suffered more and more relapses into schizophrenia and was mostly in hospital. When she came home she was frequently deluded and our relationship gradually broke down. We were now divorced and I had custody of our two girls. They were marvellous and I soon realised that they were much more capable than I

73

had realised; having to cope made them stronger. They came up with rotas of who did what as I struggled to get home from the endless – and mostly useless –meetings at the ministry in time to have dinner together.

By pure chance, at a course I was on, I met a wonderful and beautiful lady, Sally, who was also alone with her three daughters, having been widowed in her thirties. It was love and I found the rapport denied to Margaret and I as her terrible illness had taken over. We decided to get together. Five daughters, how would I ever get into the bathroom? But hers were older and were soon off to study, so there was just Sally and I and my two. We were to have our first holiday and I suppose our honeymoon together as a newly formed family, in the Dordogne. The ferry wasn't until the evening and I still drove the Hillman Minx, which now had a new engine.

I was worried that a couple of the tyres were worn, so that afternoon I popped down to the garage to get them checked out. Two had to be changed and the mechanic said that in changing the tyres he had seen a slight looseness in the wheels, the wheel bearings needed changing. 'Ah,' I said, 'better do it now then because I'm going on a long drive through France to the Dordogne tomorrow.' He shook his head. 'Unfortunately I can't. It'll take me an hour or so and I'm fully booked up for the rest of the afternoon. Anyway, they'll probably get you there and back. Come in when you get home.'

'Do you have the bearings in stock?' He checked, and found he had. 'Give me a couple of them to take with me – just in case.' I bought them and they were surprisingly small, the size of a cigarette packet. I put them in my coat pocket and dashed home, as by now it was past time to go to the ferry port.

I picked up Sally, Suzie and Sarah, drove to Portsmouth and boarded the overnight ferry to Saint-Malo. Early the next morning, on the open road through northern France, heading for our holiday in the sunny south, they all fell asleep. Then, I heard a strange noise. A metallic rumbling noise that disappeared at constant speed but recurred when accelerating or decelerating. I kept quiet – I am a great believer that things heal up if you don't take too much notice. Unfortunately, there was no sign of healing in the next half hour and then Sally woke up and heard it too. She was worried as to what it was. I confessed I thought it might be the wheel bearings. But I told her that the English mechanic said they would probably last for the duration of our trip.

It was now Saturday morning and a bank holiday weekend in France, with everything closed until Tuesday. Sally thought we should

74

get it checked out and find out what the problem was. We pulled off the main road into a village and found a small family garage. I stopped outside and we trooped into his workshop. It was three minutes to noon on a holiday weekend; the mechanic was scrubbing his oily hands and said that unfortunately he was just closing for the long weekend. But when he saw the forlorn expressions on the faces of the three females in my party he relented, listened as I described the noise from my car, and asked me to bring it in. He jacked it up and we stood around nervously for the diagnosis. It did not take long.

He turned to me. 'Monsieur, c'est les roulements, ils sont finis.' I had not known the French word for wheel bearings, but now I did. It was roulements. In my basic French, I pleaded, 'Can you do it for us, please, we are on a long journey and unless it's repaired we will have to find a hotel and stay over here until Tuesday – missing much of our holiday.' We stared pleadingly at him, our future for the next four or five days in his hands. 'Well, monsieur, although I am now closed for the long weekend I do feel sorry for you and I would have done it for you. But regrettably Le 'Illman Minx is not well known here in France, in fact I have never worked on one before and I do not have roulements for Le 'Illman Minx. They would have to come from Paris and I cannot order them now until Tuesday and they won't get here until Wednesday or Thursday, when I would be 'appy to put them in.'

He started to take off his overall, content that he had at least shown willing – but what he badly wanted was to get home for a bottle of red wine and a good lunch. He had an absolutely cast-iron excuse, he didn't have any roulements for Le 'Illman Minx. My spirits sank with the realisation that we might spend the best part of the first week of our holiday in this non-descript little village in northern France, just off the main road south. Everyone looked sad; I thrust my hands deep into my pockets. What to do? But my hands touched upon two small cardboard packets.

It was the bearings, the roulements. I cried out triumphantly. 'Monsieur, I have Hillman Minx roulements here, dans ma poche.' He looked at me in disbelief – I must surely be making it up, it was a trick. Who in their right mind carries roulements around with them in their pocket? I handed them over. He saw that they were the genuine article and was dumbfounded. 'Ah, les Anglais,' he cried, shaking his head and pulling his overalls back on. In an hour we were once again heading south.

Japan: A 'Private' egg? (1978)

It was another international fisheries science conference in Tokyo and I was a keynote speaker from the London Chief Scientists' Group, together with other foreign scientists. The hall didn't look full but just before it started the minister who was to deliver the welcome arrived, followed by about 150 people –dressed identically. They filed in and occupied the first ten rows, which had been reserved. They were from China and they were all wearing the same Chairman Mao suits. Those that wore glasses had identical glasses.

They did not react in any way to the welcoming speeches nor, when my time came, to my presentation. I was told later that they did not understand English at all. I have delivered poor speeches before, but it was disconcerting to look out into an audience that was blankly uncomprehending, and all wearing the same clothes.

The Japanese sponsors put us foreigners up in a large hotel with hundreds of small rooms. We were the only westerners there and were told that breakfast was included and it was Japanese style. It would be served in our rooms every day at 7 a.m. as the hotel, although enormous, had no restaurant. Each morning there was a sharp knock on my flimsy door, which flew open, and a diminutive waiter with oiled black hair, as if rocket propelled, rushed in and put a small plastic tray on the tiny table beside the bed. In a microsecond he was gone.

The contents of the tray were always the same: a couple of scoops of rice with something fishy in it, some seaweed, hot spicy sauce in a little sachet, green tea and a plastic knife and fork. It was not my favourite way to start the day and I asked the waiter if I might perhaps have a western breakfast. The word 'no', they say, is never used in the Japanese language – especially to 'honoured foreign guests'. So they couldn't say no. 'Maybe slight difficulty,' they said. 'Japanese government pay for your stay in conference hotel and not allow foreign food, too expensive.' I was hungry in the mornings and not pleased with my breakfasts (seaweed not being my idea of a good way to start the day unless you are a sea slug), and all three of us foreign scientists asked if we could have toast, bacon and eggs.

For the first three mornings the reply was the same: 'Maybe slight difficulty.' The waiters must have then realised that there might be a new business opportunity here. The next morning, I received the usual urgent knock, the door bursting open and the waiter rushing into the room and placing the tray with the usual Japanese breakfast on the tiny bedside table. But three minutes later there was another urgent knock, the same waiter again rushed into the room and this time paused by the bed and breathlessly asked, 'Would you like a private egg?'

China: No fishing (1980)

The first British fisheries delegation to China, that's what we were. China was still sunk in the drudgery and repression of Mao's communism, although he had died three years before. Everyone still wore the same clothes, the same glasses and no one talked frankly. The regime existed on a web of lies. After the obligatory meetings with the bigwigs in Beijing, which were endless and unproductive, we were at last released to the real world. The first stop was the main fishing port of Guangdong. We were looking forward to seeing it as it was said to be huge. It was: there were fishing vessels as far as the eye could see, each tied up to the next.

You could have walked way out to sea on the boats. This is something we had never seen before; in most fishing ports, many of the vessels are naturally out fishing. We were taken to a vast meeting room where we sat around on settees, drinking tea. We made presentations on the fishing industry in Britain and I talked about the scientific research programmes that we were funding. Then it was their turn – lots of facts and figures but no mention of the vast fleet tied up outside our windows. It was as if that fleet had nothing to do with what we were talking about. We thanked them warmly and asked the obvious question: 'Why is the fleet all tied up, and why is no one fishing?'

There was a flutter of nervousness across the room. No one wanted to answer; they all looked at the boss. He paused and lit a cigarette. After giving the question deep thought, he said, 'This is due to the weather.' We looked out of the window at the hundreds of boats; it was a perfect day – no wind, no storms. It didn't make any sense but there was no point in pressing the matter: we had the official explanation.

There was a 'banquet' every night we were there, but on this occasion one of the fishermen's leaders was invited and was sitting next to me. He spoke a little English so I thought I might risk it, as we were far from the boss, who was sitting next to the leader of our delegation. I said to the fishermen's leader that I was puzzled that, in such perfect weather conditions, all the fishing vessels were tied up and no fishing was taking place. He glanced along the table; there were no bigwigs nearby. 'Troublesome,' he said. They liked that word. 'Last week Ministry of Energy greatly increase price of fuel but Ministry of

Fisheries not increase price we get for our fish. So we stop. If go out we will lose money, the fuel will cost more than the fish we bring back.'

Eventually the two ministries talked, but in the meantime, everything stopped until that bureaucratic meeting took place. This often happened in centrally controlled economies. These clever people were stuck with a dysfunctional system, where armies of bureaucrats decide what the price is of everything from fuel to fish to shoes. A free market does this itself, mostly efficiently and silently. China realised that later.

That night we were taken to the railway station to go to our next port, Qingdao. It was a sleeper train and our interpreter saw us on board and to our compartment. He explained that on Chinese sleeper trains there were always four berths in each first-class compartment, two plus two. As we were five he had reserved one compartment for the four of us and one for the sole occupancy of the head of our delegation who smirked at this recognition of his status. He thought he'd have a peaceful night, not having to put up with the rest of us drinking whisky and snoring. For our part, the four of us did drink whisky, had a laugh about the day and then slept well. We thought the train was excellent.

As we rose to face the next day, well rested, the boss appeared. He came into our compartment looking haggard and worn out, despite having the pleasure of a four-berth cabin to himself. Did he have a good night, we asked? He held his head, he did not, it was appalling. As soon as the train left and he turned the light out, seven Chinese men crept into his compartment without a word and silently occupied the other three berths. They ignored his objections completely and spent the night like crows in the treetops, fighting for space, snorting and spitting. It's not always good to be the boss.

Nantes, France: Lost in translation (1981)

I do very much hate to be late, but on this occasion, it was vital that I was early because I was giving a talk in French at the main French fisheries research institute, Ifremer, in Nantes. My vocabulary was poor and I wasn't up to translating my speech myself, but I spoke some French so the talk was translated for me professionally in London and I practised it in front of a mirror.

I drove into Nantes by car, on the late side. It turned out to be a busy city and I found myself lost in a suburb. Somehow I had got myself into a quiet road that meandered among a maze of nice houses with big front gardens and then dawdled on a circular route, leading nowhere. There was no one around, but outside one house with a particularly long front path was a massive furniture removal van with the doors wide open. A removal man must know how to get out of here, I thought.

He was short and wiry, with a pencil moustache, just going back into his van to get the final objects from right at the back. I was in a panic now, I stopped the car, jumped out and chased him up the ramp and into the far reaches of his van. 'Bonjour, monsieur!' I shouted at him. He was startled to see me in the back of his van, next to several potted plants. 'I am lost and I am late. Can you tell me how to get to the research station Ifremer?' Peering at me through the fronds of the large potted plant he had just picked up, he said it was difficult from here but he would draw me a map inside the house. Would I come in to the house behind him and, while I was at it, bring the last potted palm at the end of the van?

I snatched at the plant and nearly tripped him up in my eagerness to get inside and get the instructions. The lady of the house was surprised to see this strange man that she had not employed in her dining room, speaking in broken French, chasing after her removal man and roughly brandishing her favourite pot plant. Monsieur Removal Man wasn't in a hurry and got out his pack of cigarettes, offered me one and lit his with a big sigh. He sat down squarely at the nearest chair at the dining table as if eager to tuck into a hearty lunch, nearly crushing the plant I had just brought in and deposited heavily behind that chair.

I was anxious to get the map business done. He took another minute or so to explain to the lady why I was in her house, carrying her precious belongings and putting them down in the wrong place. Then he found a pencil from behind his ear, got out a piece of brown packing paper and drew me a map. He finished it, looked at it fondly as if it were a piece of art and then took ages explaining it to me very slowly, as he could tell my French was poor. He was enjoying it and explained every nuance of the journey. He told me where I would see a boulangerie, to turn right at the bicycle shop and in detail how to avoid new road works.

If I interrupted for clarification, he reverted to the beginning of his discourse, and he kept repeating much of the route, back to the boulangerie. Madame was now becoming more interested in this strangely agitated Englishman in her dining room and asked me to sit down and have a coffee now that the van was unloaded. I was jumping up and down with impatience but I had to seem polite and grateful. I declined, thanked them both and ran back into the street, where my car engine was still running. Now I was cutting it fine. I found the boulangerie and the bicycle shop and then, avoiding the road works, emerged into a big square with a large round building in front of me. It was the administration building of the University of Nantes. He hadn't mentioned that. I was lost again.

A young man of about twenty was walking past the car, just starting to mount the steps in front of the building. He was carrying a heavy envelope. I shouted out to him rather rudely through the open window and he turned and came back down the steps. I asked him if he knew of the research laboratory Ifremer. He did. He came over to my car and I showed him the removal-man map. He took it and set it on top of his big envelope, resting it on the ledge of my car door so as to sketch in the last bit of my journey. Now I was very late and I imagined everyone assembling to hear the seminar by the speaker from the Chief Scientists' Group in Britain – which was even going to be in French. Except the speaker wasn't there.

He finished the map; I grabbed it from him, put my foot down hard and, tyres screeching, accelerated off, shouting 'Merci, merci beaucoup!' As I sped away, now mad with anxiety, I heard him shout back and thought he was saying the usual response to a thank you, 'Pas du tout'. But when I got to Ifremer I realised with horror he hadn't been saying that. He was shouting that I had taken not only the map but the thick envelope on which he had rested it. Later that day I took it back to the university and left him an apology; it was his registration papers and fee for the next academic year.

I rushed into the Ifremer lecture room, still panicky. I was only a minute or so late but I was sweating and jumpy. The director introduced me in measured tones, articulating all the vowels, and I hurriedly picked up my speech, which had been, I was assured, immaculately translated into French. I started to read it in the best accent I could do– I had practised it several times, parrot fashion. I ploughed into it enthusiastically, twisting my lips in what felt to me an exaggerated way, mouthing the stresses and accents as if I knew what they meant. We are not much used to those stresses in English pronunciation but, I had been warned, they are vital in French if you are to be understood. They were clearly marked on the paper by the translator, almost obscuring the speech.

I once read of a strange medical phenomenon where people who have suffered a trauma, say a blow to the head, suddenly find that they can speak a foreign language that they have never learnt. I felt like that too. I was floating in a vocal bubble, detached from reality, forming strange words with odd accents as I robotically blurted out the script that the translator had marked up for me. Then I realised, mid-sentence – I was the only person in the room who didn't know what on earth I was saying.

After the lecture the local TV station wanted an interview. There were three of them: the producer, the cameraman and the soundman. The producer asked me three questions and I found to my astonishment that I could understand and answer the first two, though I had no idea if my reply made much sense. They just filmed it as if they didn't care anyway. I told the producer that I didn't understand the third question and asked if he spoke English. 'Only a leetle,' he said. 'Let's ask ze cameraman to translate it,' and he added, by way of explanation, 'His 'usband is Scottish.'

When I got back to the hotel that night the waitress, who spoke English, came up to me excitedly. 'I just saw you on television,' she said proudly. 'You were speaking in French!' I puffed up at this and beamed at her benignly, like one of her favourite uncles. 'Yes, I was. Did you understand what I was saying?' 'Non,' she said.

Guildford: Mrs T's knickers (1982)

Mrs Thatcher much admired Marks & Spencer. Not just their knickers, though I bet she approved of them, but she liked how efficient they were, (the company not the knickers). She believed that the government should be more like M&S: efficient, self-critical, customer focussed and more popular for it. She brought in the CEO of M&S, Sir Derek Rayner, to look at selected parts of the government and to see how they might be more efficient, more like the saintly St Michael. MAFF was told it must participate and I suspect, to get the troublemaker out of the way for a bit, the administrators thought that I should be seconded to the Rayner review team to do a review of the Central Veterinary Laboratories at Guildford.

They gave me two assistants, one of whom was of Asian origin, an accountant, tenacious and industrious. I was briefed by the Rayner team as to how to go about the review, just as M&S would have done it. I reported directly to Sir Derek, not to the Permanent Secretaries of the departments concerned, who were barred from amending our findings. Sir Derek then reported directly to Mrs T. This is the way it worked: First, I was to obtain all the financial data about the overall costs of the service, taking everything into account. Then I was to proceed with a whole series of private interviews with staff of my choice, though I was told you always started at the bottom and ended up at the top.

I interpreted that instruction literally and started with the lavatory cleaners. They didn't have an office so we met in the toilets and I asked them about their jobs. 'It's like a breath of fresh air, gov, when you come in 'ere,' said the first one. Then I moved on at all levels through the organisation asking the staff what they did, why they did it, and how much it cost, (though they mostly didn't know and couldn't guess).

We sat down with each person we met, told them that everything was confidential and no remarks of any kind would be attributed. Then we asked how they thought their input to their organisation might be more effective and more efficient. Finally, we asked what was wrong with the organisation and what was right. After dozens of interviews we ended up with the director and of course he was much more guarded but the strength of the process was that by the time we met him we had built up a massive and detailed picture of how the organisation worked and didn't work. We knew more than he did. What was notable was that dozens of our interviewees offered lots of ideas of how to improve their productivity but they said wistfully that no one had ever asked them.

One of the departments produced rats for the veterinary tests in the laboratories. We called on the head of that section. He was a senior scientist with staff, offices, and rats. They, the rats not the staff, were housed in a large barn-like facility which was temperature controlled, secure and manned twenty-four hours a day. I asked him to take us through how it worked and then we started on the costs. 'How much does it cost to produce your rats?' 'Oh, not much, we spend about £200 per month on feed.' But my accountant was not having that. 'Yes, but you are paid at the level of a Principal Scientific Officer and you have other staff working on rat production.' 'But I don't control those costs. I am given the staff but I have no say over what they are paid.' The accountant pressed on. 'I imagine you all get government pensions too.' 'Yes, of course.' 'Then how about this building – it's new. How much did it cost to build it?'

'I have no idea; the buildings are provided by the Property Services Agency (PSA). They provide and manage all government buildings and I don't have any influence on their budget. In fact, this building is bigger than we needed but that's what we got.' 'So the only element of costs you have any influence or control over is the feed.' 'Yes.'

We started to put this together to find out how much it truly cost the government to produce a rat. The feed was the least of it. When we added in the salaries of the staff, their pensions, their offices, the capital costs of the buildings, their maintenance and heating we found that it cost £30.13 per government rat. I asked for a quote from an external supplier for laboratory rats of the same specification. It was £1.88. It was the same with other small animals. A government rabbit cost £24.07, a private one £6.15. Even government gerbils were expensive, £32.72, when you could buy a nice private gerbil for four quid. When we looked at the buildings it was clear that the decisions made by the PSA were expensive and inefficient. They even produced a sheep dip where the sheep could make U-turns.

I suggested that the PSA budget be transferred to the control of the laboratory, who would likely make better decisions of how to use the money and how to save funds that they could spend on better science. The head of the PSA was furious. I was called to see him in his high-rise office in Croydon. He was menacing; I thought at one point he might try to throw me out of the window. As I left he said he felt sorry for the Permanent Secretary of MAFF who had been passed over in the honours lists. A few years later it came out that there was corruption at PSA, involving kickbacks to their staff by the contractors. The rats!

Brussels: Seventy per cent of nothing (1984)

I arrived in a hurry in Edinburgh from London, having been appointed to urgently set up a new treaty organisation called NASCO (the North Atlantic Salmon Conservation Organization), which was charged with conserving the migratory North Atlantic salmon stocks through international cooperation. The funding was to come, in proportion to their catch, from all the countries surrounding the North Atlantic, ranging from US and Canada through Greenland, Iceland, the Faroe Islands, Norway, Finland, Sweden and all salmon-producing countries in the then European Economic Community (Denmark, France, Ireland, and the UK). The USSR had significant salmon stocks but had not joined the treaty. I was told that an account was open for the new international organisation at the Royal Bank of Scotland in Edinburgh.

To set up a new international body from scratch I needed funds for an office, supplies, a secretary, office equipment, travel and to pay myself the agreed salary. At the bank headquarters I was royally received by the manager in their prestigious Georgian townhouse in St Andrew Square. They were pleased to have the only international treaty organisation headquartered in Scotland as their client. 'Yes, sir, there is an account open for your new organisation.' I was relieved. 'Excellent, I will need to withdraw funds today to set up everything. How much is in the new account?' There was a slight pause, a shuffling of papers. 'Nothing,' came the reply.

I phoned Gudmundur, the new President of NASCO, in Iceland, and explained that I had now arrived in Edinburgh to start up but there was no money. 'Ah, you will have to request it from each country using the sharing formula we have agreed,' he advised. I phoned them in alphabetical order, starting with Canada. They told me to send an invoice on official headed paper, but said that on receipt of an invoice it might take weeks or months to process, due to government procedures for new payments. I didn't have headed notepaper nor any typewriters nor any staff. There was no money to procure these necessities. The only way forward was to run the new organisation from my own pocket.

I bought supplies, office equipment and hired a secretary. I was offered a room free by the Scottish government, who were pleased that Scotland had been chosen as the headquarters, but they made it clear that this was temporary. Phone calls to Norway and the US took much the same course: I needed to submit an invoice on official stationery and send it to them. After that it might take weeks or months to process, as we were a completely new international body.

After the first month I used up some my savings paying for everything from my own pocket. Then came the first month's salary for my new secretary. That was one thing, but how do you pay your own salary from your own pocket? I prepared my salary statement but had to borrow the money to pay myself. The bank said they wouldn't lend to NASCO as there was no track record and no credit status, and they didn't want to sue eight or ten governments if no payments arrived. No funds came in from any governments even though I had created and paid for official notepaper and invoiced them all.

I went back home to London most weekends and after four months my wife, Sally, became suspicious: 'What is this new job you have in Edinburgh?' she said. 'There seems to be a lot of our money going out and we are more and more in overdraft but there's nothing coming in. You said it was a decent salary.' I phoned the president again and said that unless I received funds shortly I would be personally going bankrupt and have to close the new international organisation and go home to London. He said he was trying to push things in Iceland but that it was a totally new payment category and had to go through their parliament. He said, 'Why don't you contact the EEC. You were their candidate for the job, they should move fast to help.'

I phoned my contact in Brussels, and he said I should speak to a Monsieur Martine, a Frenchman who ran the giant computer that paid the EEC's bills. I got hold of him and explained my predicament. 'Ah, Monsieur Windsor, I 'appen to know zat your payment was put through last week.' 'Well, I haven't received it.' 'It will arrive next week for sure,' he said. It didn't arrive next week so I phoned him again; I was now deeply in the red in my personal finances. My wife was convinced I was running a double life somewhere and that my new job was a fiction. She feared for my sanity. Increasingly, so did I.

'Monsieur Martine, I regret to tell you that I have not received the payment that you say you were sure went through last week.' I almost heard him mouth the word merde. He said, 'I am sure it has gone but there is one thing I should tell you... It is less than the full amount.' I interrupted, 'Monsieur Martine, it is infinitely less than the full amount.' I thought that would appeal to the French sense of logic, but he ignored this mathematically and logically correct statement. 'Monsieur Windsor, your Madame Thatcher, she has demanded a rebate from the EEC, so there is a gap in our funds. For zis reason,' he paused meaningfully, as if I were personally responsible for Mrs Thatcher's hand-bagging of the EEC, 'payment by the EEC to all international organisations will be in two stages. To achieve this the EEC computer has been reprogrammed by my staff. The first payment will be seventy per cent of what the organisation received in the last budget year. The second payment in about six months will be for the balance due. As you have not received it I will resend immediatement.'

The phone went dead. The calculation in my head did not take long. We didn't exist last year. Seventy per cent of nothing is nothing. Next day the bank rang to say that they had received an automated payment from the EEC for £0.00.

Edinburgh: The shape of the table (1984)

I had spent five months beginning to set up the new organisation and now it was time for the first annual meeting. All the existing parties had paid their dues, so I was solvent again and able to pay myself back. The Soviet Union was not yet a member of the treaty but wanted to come to the first annual meeting as an observer. Being an observer meant they could attend the meetings and see the negotiations but they could not address the meeting unless all the other countries agreed. I received a telex from Moscow in April or May 1984 requesting the formal agreement of the council of NASCO to their admittance as observers. I called our Icelandic president in Reykjavik, as it was the first time that this question had arisen.

Gudmundur was a lofty man, physically and intellectually, but so quietly spoken that many delegates complained to me that they could not hear him at first. Gudmundur was a lawyer much concerned with international matters and I was eager for his advice as to how to handle this, bearing in mind that I wanted to encourage the eventual full membership of the USSR, so that every North Atlantic nation with salmon stocks was a member. Moreover, it gave us an international breadth to have both capitalist and communist governments sitting at the same negotiating table. I suggested to Gudmundur that we should take a vote by telex as to whether the USSR should be admitted as observers. This was the only way to obtain a binding decision of the council in between meetings.

To my surprise he thought this was too formal for a question where there was no doubt of the result. The USSR had the necessary qualifications, it exercised jurisdiction in the convention areas and it had significant salmon stocks, though we knew little of these stocks. He said we should do what he called in diplomatic-speak a tour des capitaux by telephone, speak to the head of each delegation, tell them about the Soviet Union's application for observer status and ask them to answer the question, 'How would you vote if you were asked to vote?' If they all said that their vote would be in favour then we could tell the Russians that all was in order, there would be a quick vote at the start of the meeting it was simply a formality and they would straight away be admitted as observers.

I accepted this advice and we shared out the telephone calls. I was the one who spoke to the US State Department in Washington. Relations with the Russians were not in a good state, there were several points of friction between the two superpowers. It seemed ridiculous to me that a fisheries treaty would be embroiled in these issues and the State Department's attitude was that, while they were not keen to assist the Soviet Union internationally in any way, they would not veto its application if asked to vote on the matter. Gudmundur and I compared notes after our telephone calls and no other country was concerned, all said they would vote to admit the USSR. I told Gudmundur of the grudging response from the US, but explained that they would not oppose it if we asked them to vote.

So, I telexed Moscow and invited them to the 1984 meeting, adding that a vote would be taken in the opening minutes of the meeting but it was a formality and they would be admitted there and then. They said they would send a delegation and I was pleased that the tortuous 'what if' diplomatic approach, which I was not accustomed to, had worked out.

A few days before the meeting I woke up to the news that the Soviet Union had, at the last minute, pulled out of the 1984 Olympic Games, to be hosted by the United States in Los Angeles, citing security concerns and stating that 'chauvinistic sentiments and an anti-Soviet hysteria are being whipped up in the United States'. In retaliation, the United States government issued an edict to all its agencies that they must withdraw any cooperation in international organisations with the Soviets. There could be no assistance to the Soviet government on any matter. Opinion in the US was that the USSR feared many of its athletes might defect once they got to California.

Now I was faced with the prospect of the first USSR delegation ever to attend the new organisation being humiliated and thrown out of the meetings, having been assured by the president and me that all was in order. It would surely be a long time before they made any further approach. With trepidation I called my contact in the US State Department. He told me that things looked bad because they now definitely were instructed to vote against Russian admittance even though in the hypothetical vote conducted earlier they had said they would not oppose it. The Russian humiliation of the US by pulling out of the Olympic games changed everything, he said. He phoned me back later and confirmed that they had no freedom to manoeuvre; it was an instruction to the US delegation from the Secretary of State to veto Russian admittance, even as observers.

After much pressure on the US from the other member governments, from Gudmundur and from me, at the eleventh hour they received permission to not veto the Soviet application but to abstain. It was a near thing, because blocking the Soviets in a small fisheries treaty was just the gesture that the US wanted; it would have got a lot of publicity but not have cost the US anything. When the two delegations arrived in Edinburgh there was clearly a frosty atmosphere and they did not speak to each other. President Reagan had recently called the USSR an 'evil empire'.

The night before the meeting started I set out the room. How should the delegations be seated? I had heard of endless arguments about the shape of the table at the Geneva disarmament negotiations but I did not expect such niceties to affect a small fish, if you'll pardon the expression, like NASCO. But I was wrong.

Each country was allowed to seat three delegates at the central table. All the other advisors and delegates sat outside that central table. I decided it was diplomatic to also place the Russian head of delegation and his two aides at the central table, a hollow oblong. I put the president and myself at one end, then starting on the long side on the left of the president and I, I put the member countries in alphabetical order of their names in English.

So, I started with Canada, then on through Finland, Norway, working my way around the hollow oblong down to the last alphabetically, the USA, they were almost but not quite at the end of the hollow oblong. Then I put a divider across the table, labelled 'Observers', and then started again in alphabetical order, from ICES (our scientific advisors) down to the USSR. I thought no one would object to a logical scheme like that.

On the opening morning, the delegations gathered from the four corners of the North Atlantic and milled around in the conference room. There was a strong media presence, with TV, radio and national papers for the opening of the first-ever international treaty devoted to the North Atlantic salmon. At least I knew that the US would do the right thing when the vote came and the USSR delegation would not be thrown out into the Edinburgh streets at five past nine on a Monday morning. We were at that moment of hubbub in an international meeting when the delegates are evidently in deep animated discussions and not quite ready to start, but there is precious negotiating time to be lost by waiting.

Suddenly Adrian, the head of the US delegation, strode up to me. Adrian was the vice president of the organisation. He was plump, aggressive, garrulous and short-tempered, but passionate for the salmon and an eloquent negotiator. He was angry and beckoned me over for a close word in the ear, the favoured method in such circumstances. 'Mr Secretary, I am very concerned at the arrangements you have made here. Why are the Russians sitting at the table? They are not members; they should be at a separate table.' I explained that there was another observer, our scientific advisor ICES, who did have to participate if asked questions and that the difficulties of the shape of the room and the need to accommodate the advisors and scientists precluded a separate table just for one delegation. He still didn't accept it.

'No. This arrangement means that the Russian observers are closer to the president and secretary than my delegation.' This was true; there was little point in arguing. He hinted that his delegation, (which strangely included the vice president of PepsiCo) were upset and were pressing him to renege and veto Russian attendance. What to do with all these people milling around under the eyes of the media? His concern hinged on the distance from the chair so I dashed around through the melee, moved the observers from the end of the alphabetical line and put them in the middle of the sequence of countries, after Norway, and then resumed the flow of member countries. This way the US ended up right next to the president and secretary. He calmed down.

Now the Russian observers were in a rather more prominent position exactly facing the president and with a line of sight over the whole room. But it worked. We called the meeting to order and everyone sat down in their new places. We took the vote and Russians were duly admitted as observers. A diplomatic complication between the superpowers had been avoided. I would not now be held responsible for World War III.

Edinburgh: All the governments buy a house (1986)

The new international fisheries organisation needed a headquarters. I rented a house in Rutland Square but it was not well looked after by the owners, who were in London and Manchester. I complained about broken windows, and then I kept on complaining as nothing was done. The owner, after listening to my complaints, said in an irritated tone, 'Why don't you buy it?' I thought that was a very good idea, rather than renting the place forever, and I assumed that the brand-new organisation had a future. I established how much he wanted, we haggled and then I said I would try to persuade my boss to buy it. The trouble was that I didn't have one boss – I had nine.

Each country in NASCO needed to agree to buy the house between them in Rutland Square, Edinburgh. I prepared a long message to be sent by telex, as we didn't have email or fax then. Knowing how civil servants crave detail I gave them excruciating precision: what the surveyors said about the condition of the house; what they valued it at; what the insurance was if it was owned by foreign governments; what a fair share of the cost between each country might be. What happened if other countries joined the treaty or if some left? How would we raise the loan and how soon could we pay it back? What did our accountants think? What did the budget look like over the next seven years if we did it? How would the shares of the house be calculated at the end of the loan repayment?

Then I proposed that, as we did not yet need all of it, we let half of the space out. But being the HQ of an international treaty body, the property enjoyed diplomatic status – how to let it out without compromising that? My proposal was finally ready and the telex stretched five feet long. I sent it to all the governments and at the end of the telex asked them to vote. There were three possible responses: 'In Favour', 'Against' or 'Abstain'. The Icelandic president and I struggled through the legalities and decided that, although you can take a vote in a meeting room when, say, the representative of Finland has left the room and is not there at the table, you cannot take a vote by text and, if Finland doesn't answer, say it is not there. Finland is always there, it's in Finland.

I had to obtain a reply in writing from them all – even if to abstain. Off went the five-foot telex and I waited excitedly for the response. I thought it made huge sense to buy the property, but governments hate changes in financial contributions and this proposal meant there would be an immediate increase in the short term, though the long-term benefits were massive. These same North Atlantic governments wouldn't turn a hair at spending £2 billion on arms without having a clue how they worked, but buying a house in Edinburgh? That's too domestic. Nothing happened and I comforted myself that the officials were beavering away in discussions with their treasuries on the pros and cons of the deal. If so, they were not making any progress, as I had still not heard from any government after six weeks.

The vendor was getting restless; he needed to know. Property values were going up fast – he would be putting the price up shortly if he did not hear from me. 'What's the problem? Do you want it or not?' he said. Since my new job was about negotiations between all the countries in the treaty on fisheries quotas and conservation measures, I had earlier sent myself on a negotiation course and towards the end I realised that everything on the course was about negotiations between two parties. I want to buy your company; you want to buy my house or my car. I want to get the job you advertised. These are all one-to-one negotiations and complicated enough even then.

At the end of the course the trainer gave us a reading list and I saw that all the books he gave were also on one-to-one negotiations. 'I have a different situation,' I said. 'My negotiations are always between many parties, up to eight or nine, with different demands and positions. What book should I read on that?' He stroked his chin for a moment and gave me a crooked smile. 'Machiavelli,' he said. It was good advice.

After two months with no response to my proposal, my secretary, Zeta, buzzed me: 'The Canadian head of delegation is on the phone. It's about buying the house.' At last, I thought, one government is voting. 'Good day,' I said. 'I understand you are ready to vote on the house purchase.' 'No, no, not yet. We have a question.' My pulse rate soared, knowing the man was a top Canadian civil servant with a liking for detail. I was sure his question would be some point buried within the five-foot telex and I desperately tried to recall the figures and the budgets for the next seven years, the surveys, the accountant's views. I gulped. 'Certainly, what is your question?' He cleared his throat; it echoed on the transatlantic line. 'How are the other governments voting?' What should I say? He did not know that no one at all had voted. I hesitated, hoping he did not notice the pause, and then took a chance. 'So far, in favour,' I blurted.

There was another pause; he seemed to cover the mouthpiece and speak to someone else in his office. 'Oh, I see. Um, in that case, Canada is in favour too.' He said he would send in the vote in writing and he did. The next day I sent a note around to all the other governments, none of whom had voted, and urged them to vote as the price might go up if we delayed. I added that all the votes received so far were in favour. Except for Greenland, they all voted in favour and the property was ours. Perhaps Machiavelli would have approved.

Albania: No Bibles (1987)

In dealing with the Russians as they moved towards membership of the organisation, I was becoming a bit familiar with communism from the outside, but I was fascinated by how it worked or didn't work on the inside. One of the most hard-line regimes in the world at that time was Albania. It was essentially a hermit state, closed to the outside world. I chanced upon one small Bristol company offering accompanied tours. They must have had a special relationship with Albania, which was never revealed. Sally and I decided to take a 'holiday' there.

There were no airlines serving Albania at that time, so a group of eight of us flew to what was then Yugoslavia and took a bus to the border. A guide came with us from the obscure Bristol tour company, which must itself have exhibited communist leanings for it was the only company allowed to take small groups to this, literally, godforsaken country – religion was strictly banned. We took our cases out of the bus at the Yugoslav border with Albania and the Yugoslav officials looked at them in a cursory manner and seemed to have a private joke with each other about this band of Brits going to Albania. They said that it was not easy to cross and they had to get a senior Yugoslav military officer to take us. I asked why. 'It's dangerous unless they know you are coming, sometimes they shoot across the border if they are surprised.' This was beginning to put me off going to Albania.

We shuffled our feet to keep warm in the spring sunshine; there were low hills surrounding us and behind the haze were bigger mountains. I stared across the empty territory to Albania, but there was no road, only a wide dirt track, which led to a small building flying the flag of Albania, a quarter of a mile away. The Yugoslav officer came out. He looked as if he had just woken from a siesta and had pulled on his uniform hurriedly; it was smart but the epaulettes were fraying and falling off his shoulders at the wrong angle. There was an attendant soldier in a drab uniform; they were a pair of peabirds – one colourful peacock one peahen.

He asked for our passports and explained that first they had to attract the attention of the other side by sounding a hooter, once and then three times, which meant that there were visitors. If the Albanian side had received authorisation from Tirana, the capital, to receive foreigners, then an Albanian officer and a soldier would come out of their post and walk down through no man's land to the mid-point, where there would be a handover. He said that on no account should we make any move until there was a response from the other side, otherwise we might get shot. They did the hooter signals, which echoed around the hills and the border posts. Nothing happened.

The sun clouded over, the land darkened, it was silent. The border became menacing now and I suddenly felt happy where I was, still in Yugoslavia, which although communist was not quite so crazy. Why go over there to a mad country like Albania at all? Why not spend the week here? The Yugoslav border guards sighed. After us they closed for the day, nothing ever happened here. They peered through binoculars at the mysterious country across the border, but still nothing happened. After ten minutes we saw activity, figures emerging from the building on the other side, two soldiers marching down the dirt track towards us. At this our Yugoslav officer motioned to his soldier and to us to follow him. The soldier leant down to pick something up and marched so as to be just a pace ahead of the officer. What was he carrying, a gun? No, he was unfurling a large white flag.

Soon I saw that the Albanian pair were also carrying a white flag. We dragged our cases along the wide dirt track, which showed not a single footprint from previous visitors upon it. We tried to keep up with our military protectors, though the cases slid and stuck on the soft ground. We reached the mid-point, where there was a fence with a wooden gate. The gate was being opened by Albanian White Flag Man.

The two officers met and shook hands without a sound. They did not seem to know each other; they said nothing, it was formal, cold. The Yugoslav officer handed over our eight passports and clicked his heels. The Albanian officer turned and without acknowledging us made his way back towards the Albanian side. The Yugoslav officer looked at us pityingly and turned back to his side of the border, his soldier now behind him, the white flag still held high in retreat.

We followed the Albanian officer, whose uniform was much less colourful, in a nervous crocodile file, each leaving a long waggling score in the earth from our dragged cases. The Albanian border post smelt as if had only just been opened after the winter. It was dank and shabby, with a corrugated iron roof and rusting tables and chairs. Two soldiers received us respectfully if not warmly. They were sweating; their uniform tunics were heavy, coarse cloth, a size or so too big and spotted with grease on the front. Our cases and hand baggage were placed on a huge table. A notice in English on faded brown paper was proudly pressed into each visitor's hand.

'Welcom in Peobles Repubic of Albanie Customes Informations
It is forbidded to import into Peobles Repubic of Albanie the following items:
1. All Religous items or goods (including Bibless)
2. Pronography
3. Books or articles or guide books about Albanie (accept those producted by the Ministry of Culture, Tirana). All such items must be surendred at entry of the Albanie and can be reclamated on departitur'

There was nothing about alcohol or tobacco or drugs, the usual items that border security were hot on. We were politely urged to sit down on distorted metal chairs in this room, which was utterly bare apart from a portrait of Enver Hoxha and an Albanian flag. Two of us were called up to the table and the two soldiers worked side by side, opening each case. The soldier opening my case was careful, treating each object from my pants to my toothpaste and my suppositories with reverence (though he was suspicious of these and had clearly never seen one, lucky man). The officer looked on as if utterly fascinated by the strange objects being neatly arranged on the table, but not wanting to show it.

The soldier laid out everything from my case in neat rows. He examined it with a serious expression and then put it back in my case, repacking it much better than I had packed it in the first place.

Everything was well – no hidden bibles. But now it was the turn of my hand baggage. There were no bibles there either and the only publication was today's London Times. I didn't imagine that newspapers counted and was confident there was neither anything about Albania nor any pornography (or even pronography) in today's Times, which I had read on the journey. Nevertheless, the guard opened the newspaper wide and, moistening a finger each time, scanned every page, presumably looking for the word Albania or anything pornographic. I doubted he read English; he certainly didn't speak it.

But he studied every page, smiled politely at me, carefully folded up the newspaper, put it back in my hand baggage and pronounced me clean. My neighbour at the table was still being examined and he too had today's Times and his guard started checking it. My guy saw this and I thought he might intervene and say to his colleague, 'It's OK. Today's London Times is clean.' But he didn't say a word, he just started on my wife's bags. She had a women's magazine and he paused at a brassiere advert. Whether this was for private gratification or because it was borderline 'pronographic' in their training manual I do not know, but it slipped through unchallenged.

One of our group had managed to find a rare and expensive guide to Albania in a London bookshop, written in about 1935. This was a real prize for the guards and seized upon with delight. 'Not possible take in Albanie,' said the officer, as if he had just won something in a raffle. The guidebook to Albania was placed in a small cotton sack and tied up with a drawstring, presumably so no one had access to it, and the owner was given a receipt from a yellowing pad to collect it on the way out, when of course it wasn't of any use.

The officer beamed. We were decontaminated; there was now no risk that anything about Albania written elsewhere and brought in by us could fall into the hands of the people who lived in the country. Nor was there any risk of one of us leaving any bibles in innocent Albanian hands. The only religion permitted was communism. The leaders of the Communist Party of Albania had no doubt that the country was a paradise for the inhabitants, but surrounded by ignorant and jealous neighbours.

It was finally done and a short, squat bus, sprayed with mud like a tractor, turned up at the border post. We left the officer and the two soldiers, who by now were smoking thin cigarettes outside the building. There were two people on the bus, a man and a woman. The man wore a thick suit with a waistcoat. He was short, dark and nervously serious, but the woman smiled at us – though she did not speak. On the way to

94

our first stop in the country, the town of Shkoder, the man told us uninteresting facts in a monotone. 'Albania has 485 square kilometres of land of which 15.75 are lakes.'

We did not see a single car, just ancient trucks travelling at walking pace and puffing out black exhaust smoke. We reached the town and followed our minders into a hotel and upstairs to a bleak, unfinished corridor along which were six bedrooms. The bedroom walls and floors were of bare concrete, scrubbed clean. There were no curtains and the bed linen was faintly damp. I opened the window and instead of the hum of traffic one might expect in a town centre there was almost complete silence, just a noise you might hear in a library where people were whispering.

Downstairs we were silently served a strange meal with no smell and no taste, a kind of pasta but with an unrecognisable sauce. I asked for wine but there wasn't any, just beer. We took that but it was watery and weak. After dinner I checked outside to see if there was a library. But there was no library; it was the dim courtyard of the hotel and men in flared trousers, waistcoats and suit jackets were drinking the watery beer and talking to each other in whispers. They peered at us nervously, as if they were not allowed to, and continued their muted conversations. It grew dark, but it was a warm night and our minders had disappeared. We were told not to leave the group. The man in our party whose guidebook had been confiscated and I decided to go out together for an illicit walk to see the little town.

It was pitch dark, not one streetlight and no moon, but we soon found what looked as if it was the centre, where there appeared to be just three shops. In the gloom we made out that one was a baker. Another was clearly a greengrocer, though there was nothing in it. But the third was fascinating because it appeared to be a jeweller. A jeweller in this poor town? We just made out purple cushions in the window and on each tiny cushion was one object, small, silvery and gleaming. We could not see what it was but it must have been precious and expensive to be displayed in this way. I would go back in the morning. Maybe I would get a bargain in Albanian silver jewellery? We found our way back to the hotel through this strange deserted town with no traffic, no cars and no lights. One bicycle passed us silently.

The next morning, I knew we'd be carefully shepherded by the minders so I got up very early and retraced my steps alone down to the town centre. What was it on the purple cushions? What was it that was so valuable in 1986 Albania? I found the shop and again peered through the window. Now I saw what was on the purple cushions. It was something I had not seen for many years. Something rare that, if you are under sixty, you may have never seen. The precious items were long steel gramophone needles.

If a country can be mentally ill, become paranoid or depressive, then Albania in the 1960s, 70s and 80s should have been locked up. Actually it was – it had locked itself up. Enver Hoxha, the chief madman running the asylum, had died and his deputy had taken over – but, as often happens, he kept up the same philosophy. This philosophy decreed that Albania was the only country in the world that got things right, except for communist China, and later they decided that even they were completely out of line with Albanian thinking. Because of this innate superiority, the argument went, many other countries were eager to occupy Albania – it was surrounded by jealous enemies. Nothing good came from non-Albanian sources and there must be constant vigilance because the enemies were not only outside but also within.

Does it remind you of somewhere today? North Korea, perhaps? So, the regime there involved big madness, but let me give two examples of the small madness's. First, when I got to Tirana, the capital, and I asked for wine –Albania is, after all, a Mediterranean country – I found that each bottle was capped with only half a cork. Each glass I tried was vinegary; every bottle was off. When I asked, they explained that this was due to a shortage of corks; they only produced half the number they needed. This 'half cork' per bottle policy ensured that all the wine produced was off.

The communist party official in charge of wine production might have decreed that, during the cork shortage, the number of bottles of wine produced should be limited to the number of available corks. That way, even if less was produced, none of the wine would have been off. But he would have probably been shot for sabotaging state wine production and so, instead, all the wine was off. Second, in the fields there were hundreds of men engaged in back-breaking labour as there were no tractors or agricultural machinery. That was mad enough but when you looked closely they were all wearing the same clothes: heavy grey suits with matching waistcoats and flared trousers. It didn't seem the right kind of clothing for digging up potatoes, picking grapes or stripping cork trees, but there was only one clothes producer, the Albanian state.

The clothing factory managers had somehow, perhaps through illicitly viewing Italian TV, picked up the fashion for flared trousers, waistcoats and moustaches, (the men and many of the women already had moustaches), but they were only producing three-piece suits. It made for a formal looking agricultural labour force. The communist regime did eventually end but Albania remains one of the poorest countries in Europe. Curiously, as soon as the regime ended there was a ready-to-go and thriving criminal community and at first I wondered how criminality could have grown under such a repressive police regime. But I had missed the point: it was itself a criminal regime.

Edinburgh: Breakfast with the Pharaohs (1987)

At one of the first international fisheries negotiations I ran, the Prime Minister of the Faroe Islands, Atli Dam, came to Edinburgh to represent his country, fishing being the lifeblood of the Faroes. He was a big, thickset Nordic man of few words – no small talk– though he spoke good English. I was sitting at the table behind him at breakfast, where he was intently reading his briefing papers.

The waiter, by contrast, was short, dark, with a black moustache and chatty, Greek (or maybe like Manuel from Barcelona). Perhaps he had just been on a course for employees in the hospitality industry. He was on a mission to be nice to the customers, to get their day off to a good start. The conversation went like this:

Waiter: Good morning, good morning. How are you today, sir?

Atli Dam: (not looking up) Fine.

Waiter: Can I get you anything else, sir, more coffee, toast?

Atli Dam: (not looking up) No.

Waiter: (brushing crumbs from table) Are you going to see the sights in Edinburgh today, sir?

Atli Dam: (still looking down) No.

Waiter: Oh, what a shame, sir. Poor you, are you working?

Atli Dam: Yes.

Waiter: Where are you from, sir?

Atli Dam: (looks up briefly, now slightly irritated) The Faroes.

Waiter: Oh, very nice, sir. The Pharaohs. Um. Isn't that near Egypt?

Atli Dam: (getting increasingly irritated) No, nowhere near Egypt.

(Waiter goes away for three minutes, circles the breakfast room and comes back)

Waiter: Any more coffee, sir?

Atli Dam: No.

Waiter: (fiddles with the spoons on the table) Well, you have a nice day, sir. You said you were working here in Edinburgh today.

Atli Dam: Yes.

Waiter: Very nice, sir. And who do you work for in the Pharaohs?

Atli Dam: (now turning red) The government.

Waiter: Ah, very nice, sir, that must be very nice, working for the government.

(Atli Dam snorts, colour rising even more, seems incensed with the thought that it is very nice working for the government)

(Waiter hovers around a bit longer then homes in again on the table)

Waiter: Tell me, sir, what do you do in Pharaohs for the government?

Atli Dam: (stands up, eyes blazing, face red, dwarfing the waiter) I'm the bloody Prime Minister!

Waiter: (backing away fast, whispering now to himself) Ooh, very nice, sir, very nice!

France: Train to Biarritz: (1987)

The plane from London arrived late at Bordeaux airport, and I had little time to get to the railway station to get the train to Biarritz to speak at a conference. The taxi driver said he would get there si vite que possible. He did and I rushed into the station. It was big, with about ten different platforms which you reached not by a bridge but by going down to an underground corridor which crossed the whole station, passing under each platform. The Biarritz train was announced just as I arrived, departing from platform ten. I ran down the steps and along the underground corridor until I reached the steps up to platform ten.

I rushed up those steps but there was no train there. I heard another announcement that contained the word Biarritz and, I thought, said platform quatre. I hurried back down, ran along to platform four and sprinted up those steps. There was a train there but it was not going to Biarritz. Then I heard a third announcement about a change of platform to number nine, but I did not hear the destination. It must be Biarritz, I thought, and descended again to the underground corridor and up the steps to platform nine.

There was a train there and it was about to leave so I jumped on. Sweating profusely and completely breathless, I fell into the first compartment, still not sure if this was the train for Biarritz. There was only one person in the compartment. He did not seem to see my sweating, panting arrival into his world; he was staring into space, wearing a beret and smoking a Gauloises cigarette. He didn't have a string of onions around his neck, but he must be French, I said to myself.

Wheezing, but anxious to get off at the next stop if this was not my train, I said to him, 'Excusez-moi, monsieur.' He looked at me uninterestingly. I repeated myself very carefully, and added, 'Est-ce-que, c'est le train pour Biarritz?' I had been increasing my French studies over the last year, as I was eager to speak the language well. I pronounced the words in my best French accent. He studied me for a moment, the cigarette dangling from his lower lip. I said it again even slower: 'Est-ce-que, c'est le train pour Biarritz?' He looked more puzzled, perplexed and he screwed up his face as if he were carefully composing a response. It took ages and I was anxiously expecting only a one-word response, a 'Oui' or a 'Non'.

At last I saw that he had struggled enough, he was going to speak. 'I am sorree,' he said. 'Ah don spik English.'

This seemed to be a pattern when it came to my French skills. Once, a friend who I was staying with near Paris, Bernard, took me to meet his mother-in-law. He appeared to be in awe of her. He said that she came from an aristocratic family, was rather formal and we should just go in, pay our respects, have a little light conversation and leave. The only other information he gave me was that she had not been well recently, influenza, he thought, and she did not speak or understand English at all, but she spoke French clearly with a fine upper class accent. He said it was a good opportunity to practice my French, which I was eager to do.

We drove up to her house, a small chateau in formal gardens. We were admitted by a maid and shown into an elegant room where the grand dame was sitting reading. She looked up at us without enthusiasm. Bernard kissed his mother-in-law deferentially on the hand and made polite greetings with her, then he turned to me. I think he thought that with the name of Windsor she might just think me related to the British royal family and he might gain a little kudos from the connection. He introduced me as his good friend and she nodded at me, but with no sign that she saw any royal connection in the scruffy Englishman standing before her.

There was a silence then, as she said nothing to me. He nodded at me as if to give me the cue. I had to say something and I mentally composed a sentence in French about the only thing I had been told about her, that she had not been well. 'Good afternoon, Madame,' I said in French. 'I do hope that you will feel better soon.' It was short, clear and delivered in quite a good French accent, too, I thought. I expected a kind of formal response, which I think I would have understood – something along the lines of 'thank you very much'. But her face turned to a grimace, if she hadn't been an aristocrat I would have interpreted her expression as if she was getting the necessary saliva together to spit at me. It crossed my mind that perhaps she hated the English, but I had no time to show off my French further.

Bernard hastily signalled that we should leave and we were shown out by the maid. He seemed exasperated with me – it had not gone the way he had hoped. As we drove off, I said to him, 'Your mother-in-law did not seem to be in a good mood, perhaps she still doesn't feel well.' He still looked exasperated and looked away. 'What were you trying to say to her?' he barked. 'I was just saying that I hoped she felt better soon.' Now he gave that Gallic sound that mimics a small grenade exploding in the mouth and turned to me. 'Well, you actually said to her, "I hope you smell better soon."

USSR: The ramshackle Soviet (1989)

It was the first time I had ever been to the Soviet Union. From what we knew it was a scary super power, a hard-line communist dictatorship keeping everyone on a tight rein through fear. But we were invited to visit them to discuss salmon conservation. Four of us entered the country through a then little-used border post, Raja-Jooseppi in Finland, we were heading for Murmansk. We were the only vehicle crossing and the border guards perked up, as at last there was something to do. They examined all our possessions, even squeezed the toothpaste and put our vehicle up on a ramp to examine it underneath. We must write a list of everything of value we were carrying they said, like cameras.

Then they checked every bank note and wrote the list down on a yellowing paper form and attached it to our passport. They drew rings around each number so that it was unalterable. After an hour and a half we were released and sent off. They told us not to stop under any circumstances until we were out of the border zone, which stretched for eighty miles. There were three more guarded gates in the next two miles and then we found ourselves on a narrow track through a birch forest. The road covered the 150 miles to Murmansk and the first eighty miles were within the frontier zone. No Russian was permitted go there other than the border guards.

All this was to stop Russians escaping to the west. Any escapees had to avoid the track we were on and cross eighty miles of forest, lakes, swamps and wilderness on foot. But if they made it to Finland there wasn't a nice welcome; at that time they were returned to the USSR. Finland was wary about irritating the USSR after its defeat in 1940.

100

Russians wanting to escape communism needed to get through Finland to Sweden for safe refuge.

Our Soviet hosts told us that they would meet us where the border zone ended as even they, though high-ranking officials, were not permitted to enter that zone. We passed through a landscape with no evidence of humans; just birch trees, small lakes and banks of mosses. It was endlessly flat. We were totally alone in a forbidden zone and drove two hours or so until the final gate. A soldier checked our papers yet again, then swung open the gate. There on the other side were five men in trilby hats and long coats. They looked like a group of Khrushchev clones. They were patiently leaning on two black limousines but moved forward excitedly as they saw us at the gate. We stopped and they surrounded us with embraces and welcomes.

They formed an escort, one black car in front and one behind, for our journey on to Murmansk which is well north of the Arctic Circle. We pulled up at the Arktika Hotel. The head of the Russian delegation showed me to my room and pressed a brown envelope into my hand. I was puzzled. 'It is roubles for your extra needs,' he said. I opened the envelope and found £100, when calculated at the official rate – it was only £5 at the black-market rate available outside the hotel. They explained that they would be paying for everything, including accommodation, meals and transport. The reason for this was they wanted us to pay for everything when they came to the West.

In the Hotel Arktika, the best in town, no article or fitting was made with any care. Nothing was maintained. Carpets did not fit, they rode up the walls or missed the edge, they were stained, frayed and worn; window glass was cracked, electrical wiring was tacked to the wall and the television set on four spindly legs took several minutes to warm up before delivering a fuzzy blue picture of endless folk dancing, along with a commentary, as likely as not, lauding the comradeship of the various nationalities and races making up the Soviet Union. My room contained green, fatty soap, no toilet paper and no bath plug. The bed was never made and there was an unrepaired water leak from the room above. The room smelt of sewage, the toilet was not properly fixed to the floor and the curtains were so paper-thin that they might as well have been left open. It was mid-summer in the Arctic so there was no darkness. I had to wear sunglasses in bed.

The front door of this top hotel resembled something one might find on a garden shed, though workmen were creating a new set of iron doors with heavy welding equipment. The lifts were always full and you might wait ten minutes or more for one. The doors juddered and squealed, the lift indicator showed the wrong floor and the odour in the lift was of sweat and cigarettes. Around the hotel reception, people denied rooms were asleep on benches with their belongings in tied cardboard boxes.

People got paid twice as much for working up here, but it was a shock to see it for the first time, hard to believe that a nation that achieved space flight could only produce smelly soap. A 'superpower' that controlled the whole of the economy yet ran vegetable shops devoid of vegetables other than pickled cabbage and melon seeds. The department shops were stocked with such tawdry and poor quality goods that the citizens offered to purchase the shirt and trousers of the foreigner from off his back. Entering a Soviet restaurant that first night was a greatly depressing experience. Someone had been sick on the stairs up to the restaurant and no one had cleaned up. The door was secured with a padlock until dinnertime.

When opened up, the interior was dim, half the lights were not working and a dismal group of performers prevented conversation by playing an endless stream of material that sounded like the rejects from an ancient Eurovision Song Contest. We were 'greeted' by a muscular lady who said 'Nyet' – there were no tables. She saw that we were foreigners and there was a negotiation, so payment was in hard currency. The meal was barely edible, a fatty sausage with blackish meat of unknown origin, strangely dry tomatoes and cold boiled rice. There was no wine, no beer and no mineral water but always there was vodka and there was, happily, Soviet champagne from Georgia.

Girls hung around asking us to dance. They were pretty: high cheek bones, slim, well dressed in a homemade clothes sort of way, sexy too and undoubtedly looking to earn hard currency, but we heard stories of westerners falling for it only for a mobster to barge into the bedroom, saying she is his girlfriend and threatening violence unless you pay up. When we walked around the town we saw why the food was so terrible. The butcher's counters were a sick joke. Great lumps of fat with a few traces of evil-looking meat attached. I saw nothing in the land of the Soviets that demonstrated any taste, style or beauty. An electrical department might display an ancient and bulky electric razor, poorly made cassette radios and the odd electric plug.

The architecture was hideous by any standards, the bricklaying and concreting of the lowest workmanship. Even simple concrete steps were cracked, uneven and broken. No gardens were tended, no grass was cut, no window box adorned a single window, no paint was fresh, no tiling unbroken. Outside the hotel, we were approached by nervy young men

102

asking to buy our currency. They were desperate and would pay any price asked. Many young people were drunk.

In the shops you queued to choose what you wanted, you were then given a ticket recording your choice, you queued to pay the price at the cash desk and then you re-queued at the first place to pick up the article. But the shops were bare. People did not smile and laugh – and why should they? Here was a society demoralised and alienated from within. Its money was worth practically nothing to the rest of the world. Its products were of the lowest quality, so that even when the citizens had money they did not want to buy anything Soviet. Its food was abominable. Its service was non-existent. Its public and private places appeared squalid and ugly.

But the girls were pretty and they dressed up as best they could. They danced endlessly together and in the dance they lost themselves for a moment and escaped from the stultifying boredom, conformity and sheer ugliness of their everyday lives under the crumbling end of the USSR regime. No men joined them. The men drank heavily, too heavily to be able to dance; vodka was cheap. They smoked too much, for cigarettes were cheap too. The meat they ate was mainly fat. The divorce rate was staggeringly high.

The average wage was 250–300 roubles a month. At the official exchange rate then of one pound to one rouble that was £250–300 a month, but people happily paid ten roubles for a single pound, which was a better indication of the actual economy. Thus, the director of a research institute may earn only thirty pounds per month in real terms. We were shocked that the Russians and the other nationalities in the USSR had been living in this hideous social experiment, which lasted close to seventy years. A few of them agreed with our sentiment when there was no risk of being overheard. But by then, 1989, there were precious few people who had ever known anything other than communism and it seemed to us to have stopped any initiative and pride they might have possessed.

But the people were wonderful to us. They so craved contact with the outside world. When sitting at a table with a group of our Russian hosts there was an atmosphere of warmth and community that had almost disappeared in the west. In Russia, you had to know whom you trusted and friendships were deep. That was a surprise, too, as Russians were presented to us as a cold and even cruel people. We made good friends there. We came home astonished that we had been afraid of the USSR. To us it was ramshackle, a shambles, but the problem was that their rockets and atom bombs did still work.

Greenland: Raw fear (1990)

Greenland is immense, bigger than Western Europe but with only 50,000 people. It was within the Danish Realm.

The capital, Nuuk, is a disappointment. A rather small, nondescript town among nature's immensity, it seems out of place. What happened, so I was told by resident Danes who ran everything then, is that Denmark offered to bring to the Inuit people similar public services to those in Denmark. But there was a catch: they had to stop wandering and move into the town, where the Danes would build them flats, libraries, shops, a school and a hospital. This looked a good idea but it was to mean a major change in lifestyle and culture for the Inuit, who were accustomed to living a semi-nomadic existence in scattered settlements hunting for their food.

Although they must have been seduced by the civilised assets that the Danish government was generously offering them, it seems to have demoralised many. I was told that alcohol had become a big problem in a country that, because there was nothing to ferment, hadn't had alcohol before. The benefits to be gained from the Danish offer meant there was no need to go hunting anymore. The expat Danes I met there told me of the disintegration of the Inuit culture caused by the total change in their lifestyle from semi-nomadic to a static, settled people.

Stuck in their small apartments, they must have died of boredom, even though they had a supermarket and a school and a hospital. On Friday nights when they were paid or the benefit cheque arrived there was heavy drinking and even furniture taken outside, smashed and burnt to light a campfire which they sat around and cooked seal meat, as in the old days. The urge to go down to the coast and catch a seal was still powerful but there was nowhere to put it in the small apartments, except in the bath.

There are no roads between the towns and villages in Greenland, the distances are too great and the terrain too difficult, so I flew to a fishing village Sisimuit. The Greenlandic people are totally dependent on fishing for their existence; it isn't a hobby. That night I left the small Danish-run guesthouse where I was staying and walked down to the compact fishing dock. There was a massive rock overlooking the village and a narrow path to the dock. As I rounded a corner at the entrance to the dock I found four young men right in my way. They were holding knives and fooling about, and they were drinking and already extremely drunk.

104

As soon as they saw me they became much less playful staring at me aggressively. They would have assumed I was a Dane, who some considered to be a colonial power. I thought of turning back and running but I was already among them. They shouted at me and one moved – or staggered – directly into my path. I sidestepped and he fell over. I ran ahead and they did not follow me. I sprinted right to the end of the dock but there was nowhere else to go: the dock ended up against the monolithic rock. What to do? I thought I would just wait to see if they cleared off. The noise and shouting persisted for another hour; I was getting cold.

Eventually, the sound died down and I gingerly retraced my steps, knowing I might have to run the gauntlet again. As I got close to the scene of the ambush I heard noises, but not loud ones as before. As I drew level to where they had been I saw them again. They were flat out on the cold, hard earth, all drunk and all snoring. I stepped over them to get by and was soon with relief back in the guesthouse.

The next evening, after my work visits, I walked out of the village up the hill. At that time of year, it was light almost all night so far north. The track petered out but I kept going, feeling drawn up into the hills below the mountain. As I walked into the wilderness I had the thrilling feeling that, given the immensity of the land and the few people who lived there, on the edges of the landmass, the ground on which I was walking had probably never been touched before by a human foot.

I pressed on uphill into the interior, skirting big blocks of granite that became bigger as I moved upwards. Underfoot were now mosses and lichen with patches of snow, but it was a lovely Arctic summer evening, cold and bright. I had been going for almost an hour and was aware of the utter silence. It was so quiet that the very silence hummed in my ears. I savoured this utterly new feeling of being totally alone in a savage landscape, thousands of miles from what we called civilisation. The silence grew even more strident, a strange way to experience silence. It began to scream in my ears, it was becoming overwhelming.

I hesitated but thought I would press on to the next hill and take a wider look into the interior before turning back. Suddenly I was taken over by an intense panic, it was as if there was a force telling me to go. At first, I dismissed it, but it became stronger and stronger and then my panic surged. I suddenly found myself facing the other way and starting to walk back downhill. The terror grew worse and soon I was running as if chased. I skirted a granite rock and sprawled on the earth as if I had been hit. It was just as if there had been a hard push in my back.

105

I glanced behind me but there was no one there. I scrambled to my feet. The panic was still heaving inside. I ran faster and faster down the hill, not retracing my steps because there was no track and no record of the way I had come. I was overcome with fear and half sobbing to myself as I ran down the slopes around the giant rocks. If I kept on surely I would regain the coast. But I saw nothing other than the same forbidding landscape as my heart pumped wildly and I became out of breath and was forced to go more slowly. Still the intense pressure to get out and still the screaming silence in my ears. There was no logic, only pure fear.

I began to despair, I was lost, but I kept going downhill and after another twenty minutes I thought I glimpsed the sea, and then I was sure. It was the sea. I kept on down and down and then a wonderful sight, the sea, and far below me a small fishing boat with a clear wake, steaming out of Sisimuit. My heart calmed down as I saw the boat and the panic subsided. In a few minutes more I saw the village and found a steep track, which led back down to it. It was a huge relief.

Was it all in my mind? Later I read that the Inuit people believe in animism; they believe all living and non-living things have a spirit, including inanimate objects and forces of nature. Now, I kind of believe it too.

Murmansk Night train: Blanket spin (1991)

The Head of the Norwegian delegation, Jork, asked me to join three of them on a second visit to Murmansk to set up a research agreement with Russia; Finland would also be represented. The Russian and Norwegian borders meet at Kirkenes and Jork asked me to join his delegation there on a Sunday night. He would meet me at the airport, we would have dinner in Kirkenes, then cross the border into Russia, drive the short distance to the Russian town of Nikel and take a sleeper train from there to Murmansk.

I flew to Kirkenes. It was April and a cold and bleak arrival in this Arctic town as I crossed the tarmac. There was no one to meet me. I hung about; this was the last flight of the day. I did not know where Jork was, though I assumed they were all in a hotel to have dinner before crossing into Russia. I stood at the airport front door waiting for Jork. The few airport staff came outside and drove away. Then the lights started to go out and the manager came out to the front door with his keys. He was going to have to lock me out of the airport in this cold place, way north of the Arctic Circle.

106

'Where are you staying in Kirkenes?' he asked. 'I'm not staying; I'm crossing the border to Russia tonight. I'm supposed to be having dinner with a Norwegian delegation in town first, but they've obviously forgotten to pick me up.' 'Well, there are only three places that they could have dinner so I will take you into town and try them.' This beat any other solution and he drove me into town to the first of the three places they might be. We found them at the second place. 'Where were you?' I said to Jork, who seemed glad to see me. He brushed off my evident annoyance: 'Sorry, I forgot to pick you up,' he said, as if it was a good excuse. He was like that.

We enjoyed a last good meal in Kirkenes. There were stories of a crisis in food supplies just a few minutes away in the Soviet Union and the risk of starvation for the poor. The drive to the border took only fifteen minutes and the Norwegian border station allowed us to complete the ridiculous Russian customs declarations in comfort. Then we walked into no man's land and alongside a frozen lake for 100 metres or so to reach the Soviet border station. It was cosy in a dilapidated sort of way and there was wallpaper of ancient design. But the interior decorator had spoiled the effect by wallpapering over all the electrical wires that ran up to the light switches. We sat making our declarations; again, they ensured you did not alter or add to your declarations by drawing a tight line around every figure and every item you declared. They made us count out and show them our western currencies.

An ancient bus took us to the first town in Russia, Nikel, named after the metal smelted there. It was late but at that latitude in late April there was still light, so I could just see the enormity of the ghastliness of the town and had no choice but to breathe its polluted, acidic air. Some of the inhabitants were waiting for buses or walking home. They looked miserable and ill, with pallid grey faces, perhaps gradually being poisoned by nickel.

At the station a train stood waiting. It was to take eight hours to travel the 190 kilometres to Murmansk. By road, the journey inland took three hours but foreigners were not allowed to use the road because of military installations. The train was comfortable enough and the four of us each had a berth in the same compartment. As we left the outskirts of Nikel it was through a scene of industrial desolation. It looked as if a war had just ended. The factories looked wrecked, the soil scarred and damaged, every tree dead for miles around, the apartments hideous.

I was on the top bunk and my large brown blanket fell off onto the bed of Pekka, the Finn, below. He was tucked up snugly in his bunk and I wondered why he was cuddling a large, squidgy, white plastic bag. As the train jumped on the rough tracks my big brown blanket fell off again and when I lost the blanket I got very cold and I heard muffled shouts from below as Pekka got suffocated. I decided that the best thing to do was to roll myself up in the enormous blanket, the longest blanket I had ever seen. I climbed down the ladder, got Pekka to hold up my blanket and turned myself around and around in it until it was wrapped around me many times.

Legs blanket-bound, I managed to get back up the ladder to my bunk and, wrapped like a mummy, slept well enough on the train, which spent most of the night either stationary or going at fifteen miles an hour. It was beginning to get light and a stout lady with big, beefy arms came along the corridor past our compartment, she slid open the door and shouted out something. It sounded like a command but I had no idea what and I didn't imagine it applied to us foreigners. I drifted off again; the train going even slower. Then I heard the same Russian command delivered as if from a Sergeant Major. Again, I ignored it, and dropped back to delicious sleep in the warmth of the wound-up brown cocoon, the Arctic wind gaining strength outside.

Then she came in a third time but she said nothing. With her massive arms she grabbed the two ends, top and bottom, of my blanket and pulled hard and very fast. In a microsecond I was spinning like a top, round and round as the brown blanket unravelled faster and faster until it was all gone and I, still imparted with kinetic spin, fell back onto the bunk. It was shocking and the first time in my life that I awoke into a high-speed spin. Now I knew what she had been shouting: 'Give me your blankets NOW OR ELSE. We are arriving in Murmansk.'

USSR: Communist Party Guest House (1991)

I was definitely not a party member so was surprised that they put the four of us, except Jork, the head of the Norwegian delegation, in the communist party guesthouse – a shabby building. I was given Room 21 and was astonished to find that there was a kitchen, (with nothing in it), a library (with what looked to be Marxist and Leninist books) and a bathroom with a lightly rusting bidet. A bidet! The room was far better and bigger than the room in the Arktika on my previous visit to Murmansk.

108

Back downstairs I told the waiting Russians, Pekka and the two other Norwegians about my splendidly large room. The Russians told me proudly that Room 21 was the room used by the head of the communist party, at that time Gorbachev, when he came to Murmansk; it was undoubtedly the best room in town. I was to stay a week. It was a gloomy breakfast of black bread, tea and dark, gluey jam which tasted like Dettol. At other tables I saw other guests, presumably party officials in Murmansk on business, counting out small amounts of change to pay for breakfast. There seemed to be a lot of forms to be stamped, no doubt to claim for this inedible meal when they got back to Moscow.

Out into the city in the chill of April in the Arctic I wished I'd brought a fur hat like everyone else. There was an air of desperation in the place, much more marked than on my last visit two years before. There was even less in the food shops and bakeries, and nothing much in the other shops. Men emerged from doorways asking me to 'Change marney' or 'Sir, I buy your jeans?' There were lots of people walking and looking anxious, their string shopping bags at the ready as they prowled the empty shops, just in case something came in. There was nothing to see.

All the shelves and cabinets were empty save the odd tin of a product unlabelled and unknown. I eavesdropped as a smartly dressed lady with a nice fur hat but a hunted expression picked up each can and shook it hard, trying to guess what it might be. I knew that things were bad but did not realise the food situation was so desperate; there was tension in the frigid air. Old people were standing in the freezing streets trying to sell their possessions, brooches, ornaments, even matches.

We did only two or three hours' work a day and it was too depressing to stay in the guesthouse with the party members so we wandered around the semi-starving Arctic town, sensing the misery, seeing the empty shops and being constantly asked to change money or sell our clothes. When it got darker and colder we four westerners trudged through the snow back to the guesthouse. There was nothing for us to do there but drink vodka in my Gorbachev suite. When the others left me, I got into bed and lay thinking of how popular Gorbachev was in the west, but not Russia, where he was widely detested as the man who destroyed the Soviet Union.

All week I had been tickled to have been given the best room in town. But the desperation on the faces of the populace and the shortages of food came to me starkly that night. As I lay there, unable to sleep, I became suddenly convinced that this would shortly come to a bursting point. There would, very soon be another revolution and the communists overthrown. Then my lonely situation hit me with an unnerving clarity.

Who would be the first person to be taken out and shot or hung from a Murmansk lamppost? The man in Room 21 of the communist party guesthouse... Me!

Murmansk: Where's the beef? (1991)

When the train had pulled into Murmansk five days earlier, a convoy of cars was waiting for us at the icy station, with the Russians clad in heavy coats and fur hats. Jork was first off the train and the head of the Russian delegation met him and, with the female interpreter, rushed him into the first black car, which unaccountably sped off without the rest of us. We were then taken in other black cars to our accommodation at the communist party guesthouse. It was Monday morning. I was there as the Secretary of NASCO the International Salmon Treaty organisation, strictly as an observer but that was not how it turned out.

After I checked in to the Gorbachev Suite I asked where Jork was, but they dodged the question and said they would come back for us at 2 p.m. We walked on frozen pavements the short distance to the research institute for the first meeting and there was Jork, a broad grin on his face. There was also the Finn, Pekka a short, blond-haired, blue-eyed man with a permanent grin. He was carrying the same heavy plastic bag he had lugged on to the sleeper train with something heavy, soft and squidgy in it. I wondered again what it might be that he would not only sleep with it but bring it every day to an international meeting.

The negotiations opened and it was routine stuff: what were the objectives; who should do the work at sea (mostly the Russians who operated cheap ships); and who should pay for it (mostly the Norwegians who had large salmon stocks and were rich from oil). Then we started on the details, which were to take another four days. We were never invited to Russia for less than a working week because the Russians only got good expenses if they came to us for that long. Suddenly, after barely two hours, at around 4 p.m., Jork indicated that he wanted now to adjourn the meeting until tomorrow 'to consult with the secretary and with his delegation'.

At this he left the room abruptly with the interpreter. Pekka, the Finn, rushed up to him with the big plastic bag but his way was barred by the Russian officials. It was too late; Jork was gone. We trooped back through the dismal town to the communist party guesthouse where, I imagined, Jork would join us for the 'consultations' on progress. But he did not and it dawned on me that the consultations he was engaged in were not consultations as I understood the word and they were not going to be with his delegation or me. He was elsewhere in Murmansk, most likely with Irma, who he had met and fallen for on previous trips to Russia, I was told. She was a beautiful girl and very bright, but we were aware of the risks and subsequent possibility for blackmail by the KGB.

We sat in my Gorbachev suite wondering how Jork was so daft, but wondering how many of us could resist if we found ourselves in his situation. Fortunately we were not tested. Next morning, Tuesday, we were chauffeured through the snowbound town again to start the real negotiations, which I thought should not be difficult as both sides wanted the deal. But Jork again stopped the meeting unexpectedly, well before lunch, proposing a three-hour break till mid-afternoon for 'consultations'. He disappeared with Irma and then returned for a similarly short session in the afternoon. Each time Jork adjourned the meeting, Pekka jumped up to hand over the heavy, soft, white plastic bag, but the Russians got Jork out of the room too fast and away to we knew not where. I pondered why.

Were they focussed on enabling Jork to get as much fun as possible? Might that be the way to get best deal from Norway? The pattern continued on Wednesday and Thursday. We did not see Jork alone but we worked on the agreement ourselves. We did only two or three hours' work a day, the rest of our time spent wandering aimlessly around the town – now with our own fur hats – sensing the despair on the faces, seeing the empty shops and being constantly asked to change money or sell our clothes. By Thursday, when Pekka again brought his heavy plastic bag twice to the meetings and again failed to give it to Jork, I asked him what was in it.

He appeared more and more desperate to get rid of it, sighing as he carried the squidgy bag back and forth from the communist party guesthouse. He spoke behind the back of his hand and said that Jork had asked him to buy a large piece of beef in Finland and bring it to Murmansk for Irma. Food was very scarce and ladies preferred a shoulder of beef to anything else. Pekka revealed that Jork's wife knew he was a man with a mission and she might have been suspicious if Jork had taken presents himself. So he had asked Pekka to bring it from Helsinki.

The beef was now getting past its sell-by date and Pekka had only one more chance to pass the parcel, Friday morning. On Thursday

111

evening, we were again drinking Soviet champagne in my Gorbachev suite. But at around 10 p.m. the other three left and shortly afterwards there was tap on the door. I was sure it was a prostitute and opened the door a crack, but it was Jork. 'Can I come in?' he asked. 'I have to leave in a few minutes to go to Moscow on the sleeper train.' 'What?' I said. 'Tomorrow is when we finish off and sign the agreement. You have to be here for that.' 'I am going to Moscow to meet Irma's parents; we are going to live together.' 'Can't you go tomorrow night?' 'No, it has to be tonight. You know everything about the agreement; you can finish off the negotiations.'

I was shocked at what I was hearing and said he should be careful. And more importantly, how could I, not even a Norwegian, complete the agreement between Norway and Russia? But he gave his broad grin, patted me on the shoulder and left. Next morning, over the disinfectant-flavoured breakfast, I told the others what had happened. They were not too surprised and we completed the agreement. No one on the Russian side mentioned Jork's absence.

Before we left, Pekka went into the town and handed over the bag containing the largest and finest, most well-matured beef joint ever seen in Murmansk to an old lady in the freezing park near the communist party guesthouse. She was shocked too.

This human side of this job was fascinating. The role was otherwise part scientific, part persuasion, part diplomacy and part socio-economics. To achieve the conservation aims, we started with the science, which told us the real situation as far as it could with a species spread out over the whole of the North Atlantic. But then came the hugely more complicated bit – dealing with personalities, human foibles, different cultural attitudes and even love lives.

There is the official record as written into the documents but behind it are the human stories. These are much more intriguing and complex, involving aggression, friendship, antagonism, brinkmanship, competition, anguish, incomprehension, fatigue and, in this case, even some loving in the mix. But it worked: effective conservation measures were brought in over the years and the decline of the salmon stocks was arrested. But they did not and have not returned to their former abundance.

France: The car-wash criminal (1991)

I filled up at a Shell station in Aix-en-Provence before heading down to Toulon to take the ferry to Corsica for a holiday. My wife spotted the car wash. The car was dirty after two weeks spent with French scientists visiting remote spots on salmon rivers in France to find out what conservation measures were in place and what else might be done. I paid for the fuel and bought a token for the car wash. We joined the short line of cars.

We got out to stretch our legs and a man of Arab appearance, who I assumed worked at the service station, came up and advised me to retract my aerial, which I did. He said a few words in French, asking whether we were enjoying our holiday, and then it was my turn. He signalled me into the car wash and I drove to the stop line but, due to the vehicle being right-hand drive, I had to get out momentarily to put the token in the machine, which was of course on the other side. I crossed behind the car and put the token in. The brushes came back fast and blocked my way back to the driver's side.

He was on the other side and smartly got in the car. He moved my car forward ten feet. I was not unduly concerned as I was sure he worked for the garage. The brushes and water jets now obscured my view. He put the accelerator to the floor and my car with all our belongings left the forecourt and sped out onto the main road, tyres screaming, never to be seen again. We were standing there, as if we had been beamed from space, with nothing. Passports, wallets, money, tickets, video camera, warm clothes for the north, clothes for the hot south, suits for receptions, all-weather gear for visits, diary, phone numbers, insurance policies for the trip – everything was gone. I had even replaced the power steering on the car the day before at a price of £500. Everything lost in one instant.

I tore into the garage, still hoping that it might have been a ghastly joke by the garage attendant. 'Why has your man at the car wash taken my car?' I shouted, startling the other customers. 'I don't have anyone working at the car wash,' said the owner, as he called the police. In that one moment we lost perhaps £15,000 in car, equipment and effects. I went pale; I fell to my knees. Perhaps it was a bad dream. But it turned into a living nightmare.

We spent hours in the Aix-en-Provence police station, then days without money, without sleep, trying to get emergency passports. We were eventually repatriated to a chilly Edinburgh, still in shorts, T-shirts and little else, three days later. Somewhere, that man was spending my cash, wearing my pants, smoking my cigars, drinking my whisky, selling my camera, dismembering my car and doing God knows what with the passports and credit cards. The insurers said it was the best story they had heard for years and that they dined out on it.

Russia: The Kola Peninsula (1992)

Back to the USSR, and I could tell where I was as soon as the British Airways plane landed at St Petersburg. The bumpy taxi into the terminal along the potholed surface gave it away. One of my tasks here was to spread the word on new rewards we were offering for the return of tags applied to salmon. It costs a lot to catch and tag individual wild salmon, but a returned tag can tell scientists much about their migrations. If you don't get the tags back it's a waste of money. We were offering prizes of $1000 in a lottery to fisherman who returned tags.

A Russian in Murmansk had won the $1000 that year and we were determined to hand over the prize with the maximum of publicity – TV, radio, newspapers, etc. –to persuade more and more anglers and commercial fisherman to return the tags. The banking system didn't work in Russia at that time, everything was cash, and dollars were much sought after. The average salary was the equivalent of ten or twenty dollars per month. I carried the $1000 prize in crisp new $100 notes in a sealed envelope in my pocket. The rest of my money was in pounds and Finnish markka.

At the airport door there was a man holding up a sign with my name on it. He introduced himself as Anton and said he was meeting us on behalf of the Deputy Minister in Moscow. Sally and I were to stay the night in St Petersburg and tomorrow he would take us back to the airport to fly to Murmansk. We packed into Anton's small Lada. At the next intersection he made a left turn from the middle lane but a taxi travelling fast in the outer lane hit us hard as were in the turn. The two cars locked together and came to a halt in the intersection. The drivers got out and argued surprisingly quietly. We had been in Russia for seven minutes.

Anton came back to his car and put his head through the open window, anxiously, and said, 'If I don't pay him $100 now to repair his taxi he will call the police. If he does that I will have to pay them as well. Can you let me have $100 dollars now, please?' This was no time to argue, we were stuck in the fast lane, tangled with a taxi, so, reluctantly, I opened the prize-winner's envelope and peeled off one of

114

the nice clean $100 notes. Now the $1000 prize was $900 after only eight minutes in Russia. I wondered how I would explain that on Russian TV, as the lucky winner would no doubt open the envelope as soon as he got it.

Anton got back into his Lada and as we drove off he assured me that the money would be repaid. I did not know where or when or if that might be. I tried to make up the prize money from a few dollars I had, albeit scruffy five-dollar and one-dollar notes and a few worn pound notes.

Anton said we were going to stay in a dacha, a Russian summerhouse. It was not far from St Petersburg, in quiet, flat countryside. We arrived to find a charming old wooden house, wonky, with a garden full of vegetables and an old-fashioned water pump near the front door. But inside it was shabby and primitive. The toilet was a cupboard near the living room with a hole in the ground. The smell was so bad that it permeated the whole house. We were shown a small bedroom with a narrow short bed. As always was the case then in Russia, the curtains were paper-thin, so the sun shone into your eyes even in bed at midnight.

Anton introduced us to his wife, Natasha. She was a lively girl with red hair and she had prepared food. Accustomed to the food from previous visits, I usually experienced severe apprehension and loss of appetite at the prospect of a meal because it was often inedible and one had to pretend. The thing that gave me most concern was 'salad', which is often the main course. At worst it could consist of stale leftovers mixed up with fresher things into a sort of lumpy paste. But we ate a little chicken with them, which was mostly bone, and said we had eaten on the flight.

We dished out Mars bars, which they fell upon with relish, and we strolled around the garden where vegetables and strawberries were growing. Anton then sang Russian songs while Natasha, Sally and I drank brandy. The white light shining through the veranda, the trees around the dacha, the smell of Russia – a slightly bitter aroma with a hint of sweat – and the intensity that Russians generate when sitting together made for a real warmth on our first night, Sally's first in Russia.

We slept badly in the narrow bed and Sally would only use the toilet as if she was a snorkel diver, taking a big breath, going in and getting out again before taking the next breath. When she emerged she was nauseous, as the breath hadn't lasted long enough. But we emerged on the veranda the next morning to find Anton and Natasha still in the same place. They assured us that they had been to bed and for breakfast they offered us the chicken we had declined the night before. We ate a bit, which was just as well because there was to be no other food till evening. They tucked into it with gusto, sucking the bones, and we then strolled around the neighbourhood where we were amazed to see large houses being built among the small wooden dachas.

These houses were large even by western standards and some showed off imposing, if out of place, porticos and balconies. It was an architectural shock because they were so out of scale with the dachas. Anton said they were being built for gypsy baronesses. They must have amassed huge amounts of illegally earned roubles under communism and they were now able to use their gains. One gypsy baroness spotted us and asked us in to look around. It was a huge house with a large entrance hall and many large rooms. It was still under construction and although the brickwork was not too bad the plumbing was going to let it down. Old pipes, at odd angles, supported ancient cast-iron radiators. But here was the private sector beginning. The baroness asked us if we were interested in buying the house. When we declined she offered to sell us her earrings. The gypsy baronesses had become rouble millionaire traders in a country where officially only the state was allowed to trade. Somehow, they had found a way around these restrictions.

Anton then took Sally and I to the airport. Thankfully, especially for the prize-winner, there were no further mishaps. We sat in an airport lounge only for foreigners and then a 100-seater bus collected just the two of us and took us to the aircraft. Later the Russian passengers arrived, crossing the tarmac on foot. They stared at us. It was a large plane and there was a curious dead silence, in contrast to the noise and chat of most western flights, as we waited to take off. Fuel was tight and many flights were cancelled, but at the higher fares demanded by the state airline Aeroflot, few Russians could afford to fly. We bumped along the runway and took off, barely missing the pine trees at the end.

It was two hours flying north to Murmansk, where we landed not at Murmansk Airport but at a military airport near the city. They said this was because of 'reconstruction'. A word we were to hear many times. We were now well north of the Arctic Circle, and as we came into land over the tundra, I saw, just short of the runway, an earlier flight lying in three pieces. I did not tell Sally. As we taxied in we travelled between rows of bombers and fighter planes. Murmansk is a vital military air and naval area. Our plane landed in a large bomber and fighter base and presumably for this reason our Russian hosts were not allowed to meet us. A curious ruling as we foreigners saw it all.

We walked into the decrepit base and eventually an old truck came with the baggage, which soldiers just managed to cram into a camouflaged bus. As soon as we got outside the military base, which was large with huge blocks of flats for the personnel, our reception party of scientists was waiting. We were driven to the communist party guesthouse where I had stayed eighteen months before. Then I had been allocated Gorbachev's suite. This time we were not so lucky, being given just a normal, shabby room.

Our hosts said there was a dinner that night and the next day we would go out into the Kola Peninsula to the village of Varzuga to visit some of the most pristine salmon rivers in the world. They were pristine not because of Russian enthusiasm to protect the environment, which seemed to be entirely lacking, but because the area contained military and nuclear arms bases and so had been closed to most Russians and all foreigners during the Cold War.

We made the journey to Varzuga around the edges of the White Sea; much of the driving was along white sandy beaches as the road was almost impassable. Although we were far north it was mid-July and surprisingly warm. The rivers were untouched, pristine, and the village of Varzuga still pre-communist, with the women dressed in traditional clothing and the inhabitants living in poor but well-kept wooden houses with neat gardens full of vegetables. The people there depended on the salmon for nutritious food in summer and preserved it for the winter. They held a salmon festival every year with huge fish baked in a pastry crust and a choir sang old Russian songs. The priest was young with a long untamed beard and he officiated at the salmon festival. Religion here was strong. It was a taste of the old Russia. I don't suppose communism affected them much.

Russia: Kandalaksa hotel (1992)

Our return to Murmansk was badly affected by the habit of male Russians to become very, very drunk. We were supposed to return from Varzuga by helicopter, but it did not arrive; the pilot was drunk, we were told. We had to return to Murmansk by road, a twelve-hour drive. But our driver hadn't been expecting to have to take us back to Murmansk that night and he had also made the most of his spare time by getting utterly drunk. He was now too drunk to even sit up. What to do? Our hosts picked him up, put him in the boot and off we set.

117

It was too far to reach Murmansk that night and the small town of Kandalaksa was the only place to stay. The hotel lobby resembled a dim bomb shelter with iron bed frames stacked against one bare concrete wall, half the lights not working. The bedroom was equally dismal but the bathroom was a testament to Soviet plumbing and flooring skills. The toilet cistern and the washbasin were fixed to the same wall but there was not enough room for both in a line so the wash basin was neatly fixed at a slight angle so that one end tucked under the cistern. This solved the space problem but created another; the water did not drain from the basin but lay at the low end, tilted towards the cistern, creating a permanent pool of dirty water. Had anyone been employing the plumber for this job they would have withheld the money and fired him. But the plumber was state-employed like everyone else and the hotel was state-owned like everything else.

There was no customer-contractor relationship to stop this madness. The hot-water pipes, which snaked up the wall to the shower, changed angle at every joint and each of these joints leaked. On the opposite wall, a rusty pipe made a series of tight U-turns up the wall, forming what can only be assumed was intended as a towel rail. The tiled floor contained not one horizontally placed tile – each one was at a different angle. Every tap and the cistern leaked and every piece of metal was rusty. The light was mercifully dim. Opposite the bathroom was a shoddily made wardrobe with no handles. In the room were three or four different wall lamps, two of which worked but were only loosely attached to the wall. The whole effect was of a room that had been assembled without the slightest care or thought, just thrown up to reach a quota using materials that were faulty and sub-standard.

The hotel was in a forest but the view from the bedroom window was of a rusting tank proudly mounted as decoration on a grassy hillock right in front of the hotel. The meal was memorable: chicken neck as the main course and a diseased apple as dessert. Breakfast in a bunker off the reception area did not seem to be a possibility. True, there was one of those machines with a rotating blade that held orange juice, but it had not held any orange juice for many years, if ever. And there was a glass-fronted refrigerated cabinet but there was nothing in it other than a few pieces of fat. We wondered whether there was anything to drink and were silently served a large glass, which contained what tasted like a mixture of weak coffee and tea with large amounts of sugar. This was undrinkable and there was nothing edible unless one fancied a slice of fat with the coffee/tea syrup.

I didn't ever find out what happened to our chauffeur, who had travelled in the boot, but he was not there in the morning. We drove on to Murmansk, stopping only once to go into a town with factories that were producing enough pollution to kill the trees for hundreds of square miles around. The place was called Apatity and during Stalin's time it was a place of exile where thousands of people from Georgia were sent. In this bleak climate well north of the polar circle they were forced to build a town and a giant smelting works. These works had no treatment of effluent and blanketed the region with acid. We drove for miles and miles through dead, brown pine trees before we got to the town. I asked to go as close as possible to the plant: it was a sight of such dereliction, such decrepitude, such corrosion and such ugliness that one doubted it could smelt anything. But smoke still poured from many chimneys.

The Russian government were so eager that outsiders not see such a place that the road had been closed to foreigners until 1987. We drove through the town, a deeply depressing place, and wondered at the inhumanity of sending by force so many people from a Mediterranean climate into this Arctic tundra, and to so ignore their health that the very factories they built poisoned both them and the surrounding land. Such places are so horrible, yet are inhabited by normal, civilised people. The workers here had been cheated again by the party – this time of their health. I was shocked by what I saw, how communism, which seduced so many with its egalitarian aims to improve the lives of the workers, delivered the opposite: slave labour, ill health, low life expectancy, terrible food, environmental desecration, very low standards of housing and goods, censorship, dictatorship and injustice. Some workers' paradise.

Finally, Sally and I arrived back in Murmansk and returned to the communist party guesthouse. We were sweaty and covered in white dust. I looked like a piece of chalk. I ran water to wash off this white dust, which had got everywhere. Although it was mid-July the water was stone cold. I knew that in many Russian towns the hot water is supplied by a central boiler house that pumps the hot water around the town and that it is often off for an hour or two in the afternoon when people are at work. I descended to reception, still like a ghost. 'There is no hot water, when will it come back on?' 'First September,' said the girl sweetly, as if waiting six weeks for a shower was perfectly normal.

'We will send up hot water to your room.' A few minutes later I was presented with a samovar. I made a cup of tea for us with it but it would have taken one or two thousand fillings of the samovar to fill my bath, so I phoned the interpreter, Marina. 'Don't worry,' she said. 'I have a friend, a doctor. His apartment always has hot water, you can shower there.' If you were a high-ranking party official there was a special always-on hot water pipe just to your apartment, so you did not suffer like the proletariat. Even the communist party guesthouse, strangely enough, did not have this.

The doctor, Yuri, was not a high-ranking party official but by pure chance had been allocated this apartment when the party official moved out. Marina phoned back in a few minutes: 'My doctor friend, Yuri, will collect you in five minutes from guesthouse, just bring towels and stand outside. He has no car; he will collect you in ambulance. Don't be worried.' We stood outside in the cool sunshine, looking as though we needed admission to a hospital. We heard an ambulance approach, siren sounding.

A young man in a white coat, with light bloodstains, and a stethoscope jumped out. 'Hello, I am Yuri, come with me.' The ambulance drove at speed to a large apartment block. Yuri was a man in a hurry; he charged up the steps, showed us in, pointed out the shower and left. 'Phone for an ambulance when you want to go back. I will arrange it,' he said. The apartment was tiny; a bike was strung up on the wall in the bathroom and a piano occupied most of the sitting room. But the shower was gloriously hot and the white chalk of the Kola was soon down the drain.

Russia: Petrozavodsk curtains (1994)

Two years later, I was invited to Petrozavodsk to speak at a scientific meeting. The small hotel was on the main street and it had a neon sign outside flashing red, then yellow. It might have been a small hotel in a small town in America. But it was in Russia in an old building on the main street of Petrozavodsk in Karelia, a city that had been part of Finland before the war. Soviet communism had now ended and there was an odd imbalance between the Russian aspiration to become a market economy and the entrenched attitudes of the recent past.

At breakfast, the Sovietly gruff, middle-aged and tired-looking waiter presented a smart new plastic-covered and colourful breakfast menu. 'Plis to read menu,' he said to us. The menu was unusual, divided into three sections headed 'BREAKFAST A', 'BREAKFAST B', 'BREAKFAST C'. I already liked what I was seeing in this new Russia, with its new attitudes and new breakfasts. We studied it carefully – it was even in English and clear, with a description of each option. Menu A had bacon, eggs, toast, juice and coffee or tea. Menu B had smoked salmon, scrambled eggs, toast, juice and coffee or tea. Menu C had only bread, jam and tea. There were even coloured photographs of each option. This was a marvellous step forward from the miserable, Dettol-flavoured breakfasts on my past visits.

We had arrived by train late the night before, too late for dinner, so Breakfast A was exactly what was needed. The waiter gave us a long time to study the menu and we beckoned him over. 'Haf decided?' he asked. I eagerly handed him the new plastic-covered menu. 'Yes, we have. We both want Breakfast A, please.' He frowned, hesitated, looked exasperated. 'Only have C.'

The night before when I checked into my room I was allocated a suite. It looked new. There were two small but high-ceilinged adjoining rooms with a separating archway, a heavy-looking bed in one room and a sturdy sofa in the other. Unfortunately, my suite looked onto the main street and the flashing neon sign was right outside the bedroom window. I knew I could not sleep with that and so the first thing I did was to draw the curtains, which reached right to the ceiling. Almost silently, as if it had never been connected, the heavy wooden pole holding up the tall curtains parted company with the wall, and the whole construction dropped to the floor.

I was not hit but now the neon flashed harshly and directly onto my bed and, if they had cared to, the inhabitants of Petrozavodsk could have observed every move of the rare British visitor to their town. I descended to reception to report the problem but there was no one there who spoke English except to say, 'Tomorrow, tomorrow... Manager will come.' My colleague Patrick had the bedroom next to mine, I asked him for help to try to put the curtains back up, but although we stood on tables and chairs we could not reach the ceiling. The only solution was to carefully draw the curtains in the other room and swap the furniture around, putting the bed into the small room where the sofa was and moving the sofa into the bedroom area to let the neon sign harmlessly flash onto it. This we did, but with great effort as both pieces of furniture were heavy.

The next morning, after Breakfast C and before going off to the meeting with the Russians, I saw the manager. He was not apologetic – quite the opposite. He was surly and said, 'Curtain will be reparated.' In the evening I came back to the hotel to find that the curtain was not 'reparated' but the bed and sofa had been returned to their original parts of the suite. At reception again the same conversation. 'Manager not here, will come tomorrow,' was all they said. Patrick and I set to and did our furniture removals act again – heavy work, but there was no

121

alternative if sleep was to be possible. This pattern persisted throughout the entire week.

Each morning a brush with the manager resulted in an even surlier 'Curtains will be reparated' and each evening we returned to the hotel to find the curtains had not been reparated but bed and sofa had been put back into their allocated rooms. This was followed every night by exhausting bed-and-sofa moving by Patrick and me. On Friday evening I returned to the hotel to check out and then head for the railway station, where we were to take the sleeper train to St Petersburg. The whole Russian delegation, ten of them, came to the hotel to see us off at the station. I picked up my bags and went to reception.

The manager was there, which was unusual at that time of the day. I said I was checking out. 'You must pay for curtains,' he barked. 'No, I will certainly not be paying for any curtains,' I said. 'It is you who should be paying me for moving furniture every night.' He dismissed this as a remark unworthy of the slightest interest and simply repeated that I must pay for the curtains. Each time he said it I simply refused. This to and fro continued for a few minutes as the Russians, most of whom did not speak English, looked on. The interpreter did of course speak English but appeared to find the conversation beyond his comprehension and above his grade. We reached stalemate and I said to the manager that I must now leave to get the sleeper train, which left in fifteen minutes. He barked at me. 'If you will not pay curtains you must write confession.'

I had heard of show trials under the Soviet Union where the accused wrote confessions even when innocent and were duly executed. I was not going to die for a pair of curtains so I asked him for pen and paper. I wrote in capital letters, 'I confess'. He looked on approvingly at this opening phrase. I continued, 'that this hotel displays the worst aspects of communist attitudes to customers.' He grabbed the paper, seeming only to see the first two words and triumphantly put it into his file. The Russians waiting in the lobby looked uneasy at the tone of the exchange but showed no direct curiosity about the incident. I heard the word 'curtains' being exchanged and saw heads shaking and hand gestures miming curtains tumbling.

They took us to the station, only a short distance, in a convoy of cars. The sleeper train was waiting; we said our farewells and the Russians remained on the platform to wave us goodbye. On the train, straight to my compartment I hurried to the window to wave goodbye to our new friends. As the train pulled away they waved vigorously and I waved back to them even more so. Then the curtains fell off.

Chile: The astronomical observatory (1995)

Sally and I were in Santiago, Chile, where I had a good friend, a scientist who had come to Hull years before. He knew an astronomer and asked if we would like to go north up towards the Atacama Desert where he ran a telescope. The Atacama is one of the driest places in the world; precipitation is extremely rare there. My friend said we should go north and stay in a hotel he knew in a small town, La Serena, en-route. He would call me there to confirm if it was possible to visit his friend at the observatory. He did call me that night; over a bad line he said that the next day we should go further north from La Serena on the main Pacific highway then turn inland at the next village, which he named but I couldn't pronounce. It was just off the main road but was signposted and we should ask again in that village for the road to our destination, which was not signposted but which was, I thought he said, called Vacunars.

I wrote it in big letters on a sheet of white paper because if we didn't get to the meeting place at the base of the mountain by 10 a.m. the trip would be missed. We could be met at that time only and then travel in convoy to the observatory, as the track up the mountain was not well marked and wasn't safe to the inexperienced driver. It was not open to the public. But he said that although there were no signs to Vacunars, and there was just a single-track dirt road out of the village, the locals were friendly. If we just asked, he told us, they would surely point us in the right direction.

That day didn't start too well because the night before, as we arrived at the hotel in La Serena, like many travellers to South America, I was overcome with terrible diarrhoea. I had been told that this was likely and came equipped with a massive toilet bag full of pills for whatever might happen to us. It was so full that I threw away the outer packets and just kept the pills. I delved into it scattering the various coloured pills across the bed, desperate to stop my bowels from liquefying. I knew there were green pills and red pills in there and that one was for diarrhoea and one for constipation but, unfortunately, I didn't know which was which and the drug names didn't help. This was before the internet, so I couldn't look it up.

I was sure it was the red ones for diarrhoea so I took two. As I was to find out very soon, the red ones were to treat constipation. Treating extremely loose bowels with a strong drug to loosen the bowels might appeal to alternative medicine therapies but it kept me in the toilet all night. The next morning I wasn't in the greatest shape to find a remote observatory that wasn't even signposted, asking for directions in a language I didn't speak for a place I could not pronounce. Drained of all solid materials and not daring any breakfast, we set off.

After an hour or so heading north into the desert on a road with no traffic at all, I found the unpronounceable village where I was to turn off and ask for Vacunars. As Carlo said, there were no signposts, but the village was just four roads laid out in a square so I should be able to find the road onwards. But after driving around the four roads twice, getting more and more anxious about being late and missing the whole trip to the observatory, I stopped outside a house where an old man was sitting with a young child on his knee. I jumped out of the car brandishing my sheet of white paper and shouted the name I had written down.

'Por favor, VACUNARS!' I yelled at the old man. He looked at me, a foreigner holding a white sheet of paper and shouting out an urgent command. Maybe he discerned from my urgency and my distorted body language that the foreigner was not only in a terrible hurry but also showed signs of bad diarrhoea. He grabbed the child, rushed into the house and slammed the door shut. Perplexed, I got back in the car and, now even more anxious, drove around to the second road of the square town, stopping outside a shabby shop where a woman was gossiping with two other women, each with babies in prams. I screeched to a halt again and repeated my performance with even more urgency. 'VACUNARS, POR FAVOR!' I cried out to them.

They took one look at me, appeared to become scared and rushed off, pushing their prams in all directions to get away as fast as possible from this strange messenger. I drove to the third street and again screamed to a halt, this time outside a school where a teacher was standing at the gate during playtime. I repeated my plea – 'VACUNARS, POR FAVOR!' – and received the same horrified reaction. She slammed the school gate and ushered the children inside, staring back at me as if I was a harbinger of doom. I was desperate and my bowels were on the verge of further liquefaction as the pills for constipation continued doing what they were designed to do.

I drove to the fourth street and right in a corner I saw a way out, a narrow dirt road. It was not signposted but it appeared to be the only way out of the village towards the hills. I took it and after half an hour there were encouraging signs of a settlement. We reached it, and found it was called not Vacunars but Vicuna. The word didn't seem all that different to me; I thought they should have understood me even if I got the name a little wrong and my accent was abominable. We got to the turning to the observatory and joined the small convoy to the top. When we got out of the car it was into a light so blindingly bright, so soaked in ultraviolet, that it was as if we had stepped out onto another planet.

But the first thing I was desperate to see at the observatory was not the stars but the toilet. After a wonderful visit both to the toilet and to this other world we took the same road back. Gingerly, I entered the same village and drove around the square, wondering whether there was a posse of citizens waiting for me. But why had they reacted so badly to my reasonable request for directions, 'VACUNARS, POR FAVOR!' I did not know and in any case the village was deserted now with the front doors closed.

Back in Santiago a few days later Carlos asked me about the trip. I said that it was marvellous but told him of my strange experience in the little village. 'What did you say to them?' he asked me suspiciously. I just said 'Vacunars, por favor! Admittedly, Carlos, I was in a great hurry and shouting it loudly, reading from a piece of paper I had written it on so as to get it right. I also had bad diarrhoea,' I added helpfully, hoping to explain my poor accent. 'You weren't asking for directions to Vicunas,' he told me. 'You were rushing around the village, brandishing a piece of paper and shouting out in a foreign accent, "GET VACCINATED!"'

Buckingham Palace: The wrong drink (1995)

In my office sat a group of Norwegian students who were visiting Edinburgh. My secretary, Zita, buzzed me, interrupting my boring presentation to them, though I had told her I wouldn't take any calls. 'There's a gentleman on the phone, I didn't catch his name, it sounds quite long, but it's Commander something or other and he insisted on talking to you personally.' I took the call rather brusquely, sounding like Basil Fawlty. 'Yes. Yes. Who is it? Sorry I'm in a bit of a hurry at the moment.'

Back came dulcet and cultured tones I didn't recognise, talking slowly and precisely. 'Good afternoon to you, Dr Windsor... I have been asked to telephone you...' (Oh, get on with it, I thought, as he droned on.) '...Because the Queen and the Duke of Edinburgh wondered if you would kindly like to join them for luncheon on the fifteenth of April at one o'clock?' Suddenly I morphed into a man of charm, with all the time in the world. I tried to recover. 'Ooh, ahh, umm, yes. Yes, how very kind. I am sure I can make that date.' 'Good,

good,' he said. 'We will send you an invitation.' 'But... but...' I stammered, as a hundred questions flooded into my head. But he had rung off.

So it was that six of us, from different backgrounds and jobs, hung around the gates to the palace on 15 April so we would arrive at precisely 12:50 p.m. as stated on the thick gold-embossed invitation card. I was ridiculously early and walked around in circles for twenty-five minutes – I was exhausted by the time I arrived. When the exact time came I was at the front gate and the policeman sent me across the courtyard, pointing to an enormous wooden door to the far right of the palace façade. It was at least five times my height and ten times my width. As I crossed the expanse of white gravel I wondered how on earth I was going to open it, but when I got up close I saw a small door, of the same pattern and colour, set in the massive door, and there was a knocker. I knocked and it opened at once, I passed through and another policeman pointed me to a grander door to the side and back of the palace.

As I got there I saw that two of the other guests had already arrived; three more came in through the massive wooden door right behind me. There were six of us arriving at precisely the requested time. The door swung open and the same cultured tones I had heard on the phone greeted us. We walked in one at a time, each giving our name. He shook the hand of each in turn and introduced himself as the head of the household. The next bit impressed me greatly, as I am hopeless at it and he was splendid. In a circle in front of him were six people he had never met before who had each just given him their name.

He swung around. 'Let me make the introductions,' he said. 'Miss B this is the Bishop of X, Bishop of X this is Miss B. Dr Windsor this is the Vice Chancellor of Y, Vice Chancellor this is Dr Windsor, this is Miss B,' and so on. If you calculate it you have to recall six names of people you have never met before, link them each to a face in a second, fix them in your mind and then, if my maths is right, make fifteen pairs of introductions. He did this effortlessly. A footman took our coats and of course most of the guests wanted to use the toilets – nervous bladders. I was shown to one with a magnificent wrought-iron cistern high on the wall and consequently a long chain with a heavy brass handle which swung like a pendulum after you pulled it, nearly knocking you out. Curiously, though, there was no lock on the door.

I discovered later that the Queen and Duke of Edinburgh, at least at that time, invited a deliberately mixed group of people for lunch every three months, but I had no idea, with my table manners, how I had got

126

onto the list. It was like the start of one of those jokes: there was a ballet dancer, a trade unionist, a bishop, a jockey, a university vice chancellor and me. We arrived together at the appointed hour and filed into a room where a duchess with enormous bosoms and a deep, resonant voice greeted us. 'Would shyou like a drink?' she said, her bosoms wobbling in tune. The bishop was in front of me and he asked for a gin and tonic. I, knowing that alcohol seems to have more effect on me at lunchtime and not wanting to appear too silly straightaway, asked for sparkling water.

The bishop, the woman trade unionist and I stood together for a few moments and there was a swish of air at ground level as four corgis rushed in, followed by the queen and the duke. He joined my group and the queen joined the ballet dancer, the jockey and the vice chancellor. Our drinks came and were handed to us; mine and the bishop's looked the same, nice and fizzy with ice and lemon. I took a sip and felt a nice warm glow in my throat, the glow you get as a strong G&T slips down. The bishop looked disgruntled. He sipped twice as if to check but clearly he felt that the royal gin and tonics were extremely watery. That was because they had given him my water and I had his G&T.

Not a good start for him but worse was to come. We talked about Ireland and the Troubles there. I knew President Clinton was coming to London that afternoon and asked the duke about the visit. 'Yes, he's coming to have tea with the queen this afternoon. I believe he intends to sort out the Troubles in Ireland for us.' He said this with a knowing emphasis, suggesting that this was the last thing he expected President Clinton to achieve. 'And I am told Mrs Clinton is going to talk to our women about women's rights, goodness knows why.' The woman trade unionist bristled and said she was glad that Mrs Clinton was going to address women's issues, there was a lot to do to promote female equality in the workplace. But this got the Duke going too, he said he thought that a woman was a woman and that was all there was to it.

The bishop, a pompous man, made a lame remark that nevertheless he hoped the Troubles in Ireland would soon be sorted out. The duke was on to him: 'Well, I am not sure if it's that easy. The Troubles in Ireland are all due to religion, aren't they bishop?' The poor bishop, having received a G&T containing neither gin nor tonic (but with ice and lemon), now faced the duke blaming him and his ilk for the Irish Troubles. Fortunately, before he spluttered a reply, lunch was called.

I sat opposite the queen and next to the duke; on my other side I found that the guest was a jockey. The duke was great fun and we laughed through the meal; I didn't notice the rest of the table but it

127

seemed frosty. Of course, after every course you were supposed to turn and talk to the person on your other side so occasionally the Duke talked to the ballet dancer and I talked to the jockey. He said he was not a jockey any more but wrote books – thrillers based in the world of horse racing. I said that was a great way to turn his horse-racing knowledge to a new effect. I said I'd like to write a book one day. In his South London accent, he told me with loving care exactly how to do it.

'What you wanna do, see Mawcom, is get 'old of a single piece of paper and write down the beginning, the middle and the end of yer story. Then you just goes away and fills it all in. It's as simple as that mate.' Well, dear reader, you can see that I have tried it but the jockey was wrong. It ain't that simple.

The next course came and the duke and I resumed and we talked about Greenland and the harsh conditions there and how the Inuit people depended on the sea for their food and to support their families. I stressed to him how difficult their lives were. The duke listened carefully and he came up with a nice simple solution: 'They shouldn't live there,' he said. He loved cutting to the chase and hated pomposity, of which he must see a lot in his job. The bishop said little, it was safer. I heard the vice chancellor say to the queen, 'Your Majesty, I think we have something in common.' She didn't seem to think she had and changed the subject before he could reveal what this commonality was.

What threw me was that there was a footman behind every chair just serving that one person. We didn't have that arrangement at home so it made me uncomfortable. At a signal from somewhere or somebody, which I did not see, the footmen swooped at precisely the same moment and removed your plate. Then your new plate was swiftly placed in front of you again, precisely coordinated. I liked it immediately and tried to introduce it at home when I got back, but we don't have a single footman in the whole house and nobody else seems interested in doing it. I enjoyed it but was concerned I would use the wrong knife or fork or spoon or knock over my wine.

A politician who I knew gave me a useful piece of advice. He told me that when the fruit is served you have a plate in front of you but the fruit comes in an individual bowl for each guest. Beside the bowl of fruit is a smaller bowl of water. 'Whatever you do,' he said, 'don't drink this water. It's there for you to wash your fingers.' I was grateful because I probably would have drunk the water.

We left the dining room and returned to the same anteroom to have coffee. This time I found myself with the queen and the ballet dancer. I think the ballet dancer and I developed verbal diarrhoea, as the queen didn't say much. I saw why: she was waiting for the corgis, who whooshed back into the room. She made a big fuss of them rather than of the dancer and me, who were talking animated nonsense to each other. I knew that she never carried money in her handbag but I now know what she does carry in it – dog biscuits. She doled them out to the excited dogs.

Suddenly, she must have received a signal; she turned to me first, and said, 'Thank you so much for coming.' I guess this was the clearest signal to leave. President Clinton was coming for tea. I swiftly put my coffee cup down and said, 'Thank you very much for inviting me, I have had a great time.' I am sure that she has never, ever, ever done this but she almost winked. 'I could see that you were having fun with the duke,' she said.

Canada: New indigestion remedy (2000)

The millennium year 2000 annual conference was to be in Miramichi, Canada. I travelled there the year before to plan it but this first visit did not start well. I was late arriving at Miramichi, New Brunswick (a major salmon river runs there) and was asked to hurry to a reception room where the fisheries minister was hosting dinner. I dumped my bags and hurried downstairs and a young waitress, who was only about sixteen, was waiting for me. 'I have been asked to give you a drink now to take in to the room with you as everyone else is already there, what will you have?' 'I would love a ginandtonic,' I said, perhaps running the words together in my haste.

She seemed uncertain but headed off to the bar to fetch it and bring it to me. I stepped into the dining room and met the minister and his staff. The young waitress came up to me and, interrupting the minister, she blurted out, 'Sir, they don't have any gintonk.' 'It's not gintonk, its gin and tonic,' I said. She rushed off again to the bar and soon re-appeared, looking more distressed. 'Sir, they don't have any ginantonk either.'

So I didn't get a drink then but the planning went well and a year later I arrived back in Miramichi for the annual conference with over 100 delegates. The first night all were invited to a dinner hosted by the Canadian government starting at 7 p.m. I was to make an after-dinner speech and I had discovered from experience that, if it was funny, it helped the atmosphere when there were negotiating tensions, as there almost always were. The trouble was that I had been suffering recently from chronic indigestion and a five-course dinner, with the stress of making a speech afterwards, plus trying to be funny, was a sure recipe for indigestion.

If you make a poor presentation on a subject you know about, whether it's boring or hard to follow, people forget about it quite quickly. But if you stand up after dinner to make people laugh... and they don't... they won't forget it, ever. It's embarrassing. I had seen the doctor the week before about the recurring indigestion and he was encouraging. He said there was a new drug called Metoclopramide which was a major advance because it worked not on the stomach itself but on the brain. It sounded scary but he was reassuring. He said, 'In the past the indigestion remedies were substances to coat the stomach in one way or another. But this works in a completely different way, it helps the brain to tell the stomach not to secrete so much acid. It's new but with your lifestyle – travelling a lot, jet lag, stress, etc. – it's worth a try.'

So I packed the box of Metoclopramide and now, I decided, half an hour before the big dinner and my speech, was the time to try it. There wasn't much time – I had to shower, get changed, look at my notes for the speech and try to make it funnier, or amusing at least. The label on the pills said to take two at the first sign of symptoms. I did, and as I showered and changed I pictured my brain sending stern messages to my stomach. I lay on the bed; there was just fifteen minutes left to go over my speech, which was looking desperately unfunny the more I looked at it. On the bed the small sheet that comes with all drugs fell out and I glanced at it. I read it with growing horror:

'This medicine sometimes causes unwanted effects on the central nervous system in some people. These effects may include:
Difficulty in speaking or swallowing
Loss of balance control; Mask-like face; Shuffling walk
Stiffness of arms or legs; Trembling of hands and fingers
Lip smacking or puckering; Puffing of cheeks;
Rapid or worm-like movements of tongue
Uncontrolled chewing movements
Uncontrolled movements of arms and legs
Excessive temperature; Drowsiness; Rigid muscles
Rapid breathing; Restlessness and uncontrolled movements
Dizziness, drowsiness or weakness; Trouble in sleeping
Headache, restlessness, depression, confusion
Effects on the heart: Low blood pressure, high blood pressure
Effects on the stomach and gut: Diarrhoea, constipation,

130

nausea, dryness of mouth
Effects of the genital and urine system: Breast tenderness and
swelling, changes in periods, raised blood levels of the hormone
prolactin (which can cause breast milk production)
If you are concerned about any of these effects or experience
any other unusual effects, tell your doctor immediately'.

CONCERNED? I was mortified. When you are about to give a speech, difficulty in speaking is to be avoided and a mask-like face is unlikely to get you a warm reception. Could I get up onto the podium if I had a shuffling walk? How would lip smacking or puckering go down with the delegates, would they find it funny and think I was putting it on? Could I even tell a joke at all if my tongue was making worm-like movements and I was uncontrollably chewing?

I wondered if I should stick my fingers down my throat and try to bring up the Metoclopramide but it was only a few minutes before I had to go and what if it messed up my suit? I was so stunned by what I was reading that I could not even look at my notes. The evening was going to be a disaster. But even in this panic I retained some facility for logical argument. How could any reasonable substance not only cause low blood pressure but high blood pressure, and cause both constipation and diarrhoea? How could it cause both drowsiness and trouble in sleeping? What sort of mind-altering substance had I taken?

What if I suddenly became depressed or confused during my speech? And what about my breasts? What if they became tender and swollen during my performance? I paced reluctantly along the hotel corridor to the dinner, through the window the massive Miramichi River sweeping the opposite way. I fancied that there was already a touch of confusion and depression coming on, so two of the side effects were already showing themselves. Soon lip smacking will kick in, I thought possibly during the soup course, how embarrassingly messy.

The cheek-puckering stage by the starter. What if I got to the uncontrollable chewing stage when I wasn't even eating anything in between courses or after the dinner during my speech? And would I get a period for the first time in my life?

I cannot remember the dinner at all, I was so sure I was inadvertently lip smacking or cheek puckering that I hardly ate anything. The minister of fisheries made a speech. I didn't hear it as my heart was racing and my hands were shaking. God, those were both on the list of symptoms too. My time came. I walked, shuffled, to the podium. My notes were forgotten; I thought the only way out was to make a clean breast of it (unless my breasts were too tender).

I brandished the piece of paper that was in the packet of drugs, confessed to the audience the nature of the tablets I had taken for the first time just before dinner. I warned them what might happen during my speech. I read out all the symptoms and from the podium I mimicked them, nearly everything except the diarrhoea, so they would know to drag me off the stage and get men with white coats to take me to hospital if they saw any of these symptoms. I am still not sure if I was mimicking or if it was real, and the side effects were appearing on cue. It seemed suspiciously easy for me to show how the symptoms would look. But I could not believe my ears – it went down a treat. How they laughed!

To my astonishment people came up to me afterwards saying it was the funniest thing they had heard for years. Thank you Metoclopramide, laughter wasn't on the list of side effects. When I got back to my room I read through it all again. I found I hadn't reached as far as the very last paragraph on the possible side effects of this indigestion remedy. Metoclopramide can cause... indigestion!

Boston: Drinks on the US State Department? (2001)

Drinks were a trap again a few years later in Boston, where we were holding a meeting in the conference room of a hotel. It was normal that the host country pays for the conference room and a reception. Most countries like to make a good impression on the international circuit. The US delegation told me they would host a reception with 'heavy hors d'oeuvres' (this meant you didn't need dinner), that evening at 7 p.m. and asked me to announce it at the lunch break. I did.

During the afternoon coffee break the man on the delegation from the US State Department came up to me in a panic, saying that he had just phoned his office in Washington about the promised reception to be told that they were not allowed to pay for any reception involving alcohol without permission from the Secretary of State's office, and that permission was not going to be given by six o'clock and probably not at all. He was mortified; the Americans are a generous people and he had already publicly made the invitation through me. What would the other countries think of this? They always offered hospitality when a meeting was on their soil. There was only one way out: I had better pay for it myself to protect the reputation of the US government.

At 7 p.m. we gathered and the State Department representative made a speech welcoming us all, saying that he hoped we would find the meeting valuable and enjoy the food and drink. I was then obliged, as is the custom, to go to the microphone and warmly thank the US for the very nice reception, which only they knew I was paying for. Those particular gin and tonics had a bitter taste as they went down.

Russia: Naryan-Mar, cockroaches and skyjacking (2002)

Naryan-Mar is a word that used to strike terror into the hearts of Russians. It was a penal colony where dissidents were sent and thousands perished there. We were going there because it was close to the biggest Atlantic salmon river in the world, the Pechora. Even the head of the Russian delegation, Alexis, had never been there. We flew east to Arkhangelsk, also known as Archangel, to stay one night and next day take a small plane which ran only once a week to Naryan-Mar. I pictured Archangel, with its lovely name, as a charming town of wooden houses along the Northern Dvina River. But apart from a few wooden houses left in the centre it was a dismal place, surrounded by ugly Soviet blocks of flats.

Next morning, we travelled back to the airport to catch the weekly flight to Naryan-Mar and boarded a decrepit airplane. My seat reclined to the horizontal and would not stay upright. My seatbelt was frayed and broken, and most of the overhead lights did not work at all. It was deadly silent, as if the passengers were cowed and fearful. Nothing happened, there was no crew. Then a flurry at the rear steps and the captain boarded, sweeping majestically through the aircraft in a floor-length leather coat with the flight attendant close behind him as if she was the retinue for the tsar. The passengers crossed themselves.

The plane took off gaining height at a fraction of the speed that I was used to. It droned on at a low altitude over a tundra landscape of lakes, moss and few stunted trees. The attendant passed speedily through the cabin carrying food and drink, but not for us, only for the pilot. There was nothing to eat or drink for the passengers. I spent the flight with no seatbelt and trying unsuccessfully to keep my seat upright. I beckoned to the attendant, a portly lady with BO, and showed her but she just shrugged.

Naryan-Mar airport was a ruin from outside as we picked our way through the potholes in the tarmac but there was a shabby waiting room inside. Local officials were waiting with two military jeeps to take us to the Naryan-Mar Hotel. I have stayed in some dumps but this would

133

have taken the biscuit, had there been any. The iron-frame beds were covered in stained, off-purple covers; the sheets were yellowing and smelt of cigarettes. The wallpaper peeled and the window looked onto what might have been intended as a lawn but was a sea of mud and litter – desolate is an understatement. My spirits sank; I was to be in this dreadful room for a week.

In the bathroom, I turned on the light and dozens of cockroaches ran for cover. There was no toilet seat – well, there was one, but of thin plastic, cracked and not attached to the toilet as the hinge was broken. I consoled myself that at least in the next few days we would escape for a couple of nights when we visited the vast Pechora River. But first we were to pay our respects to the local administrator who oversaw this huge area.

His office was a big, overheated room reeking of cigarette smoke and vodka. The large man at the desk hardly looked up and showed no interest as we walked in and were introduced. He stared through us and smoked. The Russians in our delegation invited me to ask him some questions through the interpreter. I asked the official how the river was managed, what were the catches, was there a scientific programme, and was there a problem with illegal fishing in such a vast river? He stared through me, muttered five words and lapsed into smoking. The interpreter looked lost. The official had said nothing. We sat there in silence for another half hour, talking quietly among ourselves. Then, respects evidently paid, we returned to the cockroach farm.

Curiously, next door to the hotel was a newly opened private shop, which sold passable convenience foods, crisps, buns and tinned foods, so we ate those that night. Next day, we were taken to the mighty Pechora to board a boat. We were to spend the day navigating the river and pass the night on an island in the river. There were other boats in the harbour; they all appeared ruined, some were half sunken and all were drenched in rust. Again I had the strong sensation that we were in a place where a war had just ended. Our boat crept out around these abandoned hulks and for the first time I saw the Pechora. It was huge; the other side too far away to see.

We chugged downstream for an hour or two; they showed us a few semi-derelict fishing stations where, they said, biologists took samples, measured salmon. But there was no one at any of them. The landscape was flat, and in the middle of the river it was as if we were at sea. The boat drifted on through the vastness of the river and the Arctic emptiness. There were no villages, no buildings… an empty world except for birds and salmon. The boat turned in the late afternoon and now started to head back up stream, moving towards the opposite bank of this huge river. After another hour I saw an island in the river.

A plume of smoke rose from the island and there were old buildings; it looked like a military fort. We landed and found the fort to be a large structure with an imposingly fortified entrance, now damaged. Inside, a wide, long corridor with spacious rooms leading off, which were empty. Some had broken windows; there were birds and bird droppings and it was hard to imagine what purpose the building had served in this empty, unpopulated place. Many political prisoners had been held in labour camps in the hinterland who would have thought of escaping down the Pechora and this fort had been well placed for the military to monitor the river.

They showed us into a massive shell of a room that could have accommodated thirty or forty beds, but there were only three beds, one for each of us, the foreigners. The beds were iron framed, heavily corroded with rust, with woven wire mattresses. They had been used for so long that all three mattresses sagged almost to the concrete floor. There was no electricity but no need for lights in the mid-summer Arctic night. I was always amazed by the resourcefulness of the Russians, who coped with whatever was thrown at them. They got a fire going in the courtyard of the abandoned fort and were cooking salmon, fresh from the Pechora, and boiled potatoes. For a starter they brought lots and lots of the terrible black sausage, a staple always available, like vodka. A bottle of vodka can never be capped once opened.

We ate well and we three foreigners retired for the night to our vast barrack room. The Russians still had vodka so stayed up but we never saw where they slept. The three beds in our massive room were placed ten metres apart, as if to try to occupy the whole of the space. It was getting cold but not getting dark so we climbed into the rusting beds, shouting our good nights across the vast barrack room. Then the trouble started. Albert, the Norwegian, had a serious snoring problem, and his snores filled the vast, echoing room. It was chilly and too far to get out of bed, walk across the cold stone floor and wake him, so we threw things at him, socks, pants and eventually shoes. But it had no effect at all. Patrick and I could not sleep with the noise quite apart from the lack of darkness, no curtains and the sun coming through the cracked windows at 3 a.m.

The absurdity struck me, in this empty world on an island on a vast Arctic river, in a ruined fort, in a barrack room on a rusting bed, listening all night to a Norwegian master-snorer. In the morning a shout from the Russians told that breakfast was ready. Albert awoke from his deep sleep, stretched with the obvious satisfaction of the well-rested, and announced that he had slept like a log. I trudged over to his bed to collect the thrown items and threatened to strangle him. He said this didn't bother him as his wife made the same threat every night. She had booked him an operation to stop the snoring when he got home, no consolation to us his bed mates now.

The next day the boat sailed back to the decaying dock, difficult to get in to because of the sunken and half-submerged wrecks surrounding it. A jeep took us to our dreadful hotel. The cockroaches were still there. They hadn't changed the wallpaper either. We had finished our visit to this little-known river, the biggest Atlantic salmon river in the world. But it was four more nights before the next weekly flight. As we walked downstairs to scavenge for food, Alexis saw from my expression that I did not relish any more time in Naryan-Mar. I didn't realise that it showed. Imagine being banished there for life in a labour camp.

He said, 'Would you like go back to Archangel tonight?' 'Well, yes,' I said. 'We have finished our work and learnt all that we can. But, Alexis, I know we can't go back, there are no flights for four days.' He turned and spoke animatedly to the interpreter, who lived in Archangel. He checked his wallet. They made a phone call from the sentry-box-like structure that served as the hotel reception. Suddenly he turned to me. 'Pack your bag, we will try something.' I would have tried anything so I didn't argue, rushed upstairs, threw my stuff in my bag, said goodbye to the cockroaches and dashed back downstairs.

Two waiting jeeps took us back to the same semi-derelict airport and then inside to what I suppose was a departure hall, just a square of rough concrete with benches. Alexis told us to wait and he strode off out of the room with the interpreter. I saw them outside; they crossed the runway to the control tower, which looked askew, as if it had lost control of itself. I stared around the empty hall. There was, surprisingly, a departure board. But not a departure board as we know, it with changing information. It was set in stone, or wood, with unalterable information, two days of the week and two destinations. Mondays Archangel, Fridays somewhere else I couldn't read.

Alexis and the interpreter soon came rushing back across the runway, smiling at each other. 'Five minutes,' said the interpreter. 'Five minutes for what?' I gestured at the departures board. 'There's no flight until Monday.' He winked at me, and in five minutes a small plane landed. We were hustled out onto the tarmac dragging our bags. The plane taxied across the potholed runway; it didn't stop but kept inching forward in small jerks and a narrow gangway came down, almost but not quite touching the tarmac. We were pushed on. In the plane there was silence as the passengers, who wore long fur coats, moustaches and had an Asiatic appearance, stared into space with folded arms as if nothing had happened. I grabbed a seat – no seatbelt, of course.

The plane, which did not once come to a complete stop, trundled on, weaving through the potholes, and took off. I wasn't sitting next to anyone and had no idea where we were going because I knew there was no flight to Archangel for days. I thought maybe we were going somewhere else just to avoid a long weekend in Naryan-Mar. I would have settled for anywhere else in the world. I couldn't see in which direction we were heading and the land beneath us looked the same frozen tundra with lakes and mosses. After an hour or two the plane lost height and landed. Where were we? But, wow, the sign on the airport building read 'Архáнгельск'. I read enough of the Russian text to know that this was Archangel. We were 'home'. I hadn't been so thrilled since I passed my driving test.

Back to the same Archangelic hotel where we had stayed on the way out. Then it had seemed dreary and uncomfortable, but now to me it was the Waldorf Astoria, with its clean, if narrow, beds, polished floors and the absence of wildlife in the rooms. My brief experience of the labour camp area over, I was hugely relieved to be out of there. Yet under communism tens of thousands of Soviet citizens were deported to Naryan-Mar, where they lived in terrible conditions. They would have found my accommodation there utterly luxurious. They had done nothing wrong and many were half starved, denied medical treatment and worked to death.

The enormity of these crimes perpetuated by Stalin against his own people came home to me. Our Russian companions on this trip became anxious and fell silent when I raised the topic of the past; Russia itself has never held a public examination of this terrible era in its history, so the terror is still buried. Other countries have exorcised their past but in Russia it seems to still smoulder.

Archangel: Pole dancing etiquette (2002)

We were so happy to be back in Archangel, as if we had been released early from a penal colony, which we had been. Downstairs our hotel had a café and we drank a beer and something to eat. Alexis then said we should go out to celebrate our release by seeing Archangel's

137

nightlife. I was on a high and up for anything. In Archangel there weren't any taxis – everybody with a Lada was a taxi. Out in the street you put your hand up and one or two or three cars halted, a kind of Super Uber. We flagged down two cars, off to the nightclub.

Inside the dark room, as my eyes got used to the dim light I saw a stage with a pole on it. It must be for pole dancing, I thought, an entertainment which I had never seen. We were shown to a table near the stage and I was seated at the front. I was now in a play where I didn't have the script. A smart waiter served Russian champagne and we toasted our escape. I wanted to ask the interpreter how on earth we had managed to get out of Naryan-Mar but the lights dimmed a beautiful young lady took the stage. What she did with and on that pole was a revelation to me. I was engulfed by a sensation of well-being.

A few hours ago it had seemed inevitable, I would be spending three days with nothing to do in a cockroach-infested bedroom with peeling wallpaper, in a desperately miserable prison camp town, looking out on a sea of frozen mud and eating stale black sausage. But here we were, drinking champagne and watching a beautiful girl dance. What a miraculous change of fortune. But the next bit didn't go so well. After the pole dance she came over to our table and started to dance close to me. As the dance proceeded she came ever closer, her breasts and bottom brushing against me. She left to applause, none more enthusiastic than mine. I had downed a lot of champagne and was still hugely excited by our implausible escape.

Then she returned to our table and kind of curtseyed to me as if to show that her act had ended. I clapped enthusiastically again but she didn't seem too pleased. Something was missing. What I didn't know was that, according to Pole Dance Club Etiquette, one was supposed to tip the dancer by stuffing high-denomination dollar notes into the top of her knickers. But Alexis evidently knew and rapidly produced a note on my behalf.

I thought he tucked it in further down than strictly necessary to hold it in the elastic. The young lady danced off again but a few seconds later a burly man with a shaven head and a shiny black suit came up to our table. He didn't go to me but to Alexis. There was a sharp conversation in which Alexis was reprimanded for something, I didn't know what. The atmosphere grew tense. Alexis dug into his wallet again and drew out another high-denomination dollar note and handed it to shiny-suit man.

We left and returned to the hotel. I was tired and drunk but still happy to get into my nice Archangel bed. The next morning, I wanted to untangle a couple of things. First, how had we got on a flight to Archangel when there weren't any for four days, and second, what happened at the nightclub to cause the threatening atmosphere after the dance? Was it something I had done? As we flew back to Murmansk he, reluctantly, let me into the secrets. At Naryan-Mar airport they had gone to the air traffic control tower and asked if there were any flights passing overhead that night, heading for Archangel. This was not a well-travelled route but there was one flight very soon, as it happened, going to Archangel from Siberia. It did not stop at Naryan-Mar... ever. They plied the air traffic controller with dollar bills, like the pole dancer, though presumably not in his knickers.

When the cash amount offered reached high enough the air traffic controller radioed the captain of the now overhead aircraft and ordered him to land at Naryan-Mar. No reason given nor expected, this was Russia, after all. The flight as it landed was further ordered not to stop engines but to taxi to the terminal, pick up five passengers and go on its way. So, out there in the Wild East a plane could be plucked from the sky at will and ordered to change its plans, if you have enough hard currency. I will be forever grateful.

As for the nightclub, the dancer had focussed on me as, she assumed, that I was the host. After all, I was the oldest, with silvery hair, and I looked foreign and therefore rich. I know that I also looked rather pleased with myself but she did not to know that this was mostly because I had just avoided a sentence in Naryan-Mar. As for the dispute and our having to leave in a hurry, it seems that when Alexis tucked US dollars into the dancer's knickers, he unfortunately tucked them a little bit too far south. In the delicate politesse of the pole dancing world this was bad etiquette. Shiny-suit man had demanded a large supplement – or, he insinuated, we might get beaten up. We fell short and were rightly thrown out of the pole-dancing club.

Argentina: How to marry your brother-in-law (2006)

My brother-in-law, Peter, wanted to go to Antarctica. He asked his wife – my sister, Judy – if she would go with him. 'No,' she told him. 'The voyage would be too rough.' He asked if I would go. I was keen and I asked my wife if she wanted to. She said, 'No, it would be too cold.' That left the two of us and we arrived first in Buenos Aires to stay for a night or two before flying south to Ushuaia, the southernmost city in the world, to board the ship for Antarctica. The taxi driver drove insanely fast from the airport taking no notice of us shouting at him to slow down and I was relieved to be dropped at the hotel shown on our voucher, the Lafayette.

The desk clerk, weird and miserable on first acquaintance, said he had no record of a booking for us. I had been in Buenos Aires before and said to my brother-in-law, 'Don't worry, this is par for the course, he is trying to cheat us into paying again. I will refuse to budge.' The miserable receptionist kept on insisting that they didn't have a booking for us and they were full. It was New Year's Eve and mid-summer too. I stood at the desk for twenty minutes, insisting that he provide us with the two rooms we had paid for. He ignored me for much of the time but I just stood there. Other clients checked in and out but still I just stood there.

After twenty minutes more he suddenly came out of his depression announced that they would let us have one room with a double bed. I said no, I wanted two rooms, but I was beginning to be worn down, it's a long way from London to Buenos Aires and we were both exhausted. Perhaps my brother-in-law and I would have to sleep together. The clerk slapped a form on the desk and said, 'Please to fill form for both of you.' Still not ready to back down from my two rooms position I thought it best to keep him happy by doing the paperwork. It was a strange form, not on hotel paper but on government paper headed 'Declaration to Ministry of Foreign Affairs, Argentina'.

It asked me to fill in the names and passport numbers for me and the others in my party. I filled in the form for me and then below for my brother-in-law. At the bottom of the form was the question 'Are you married?' I put 'Yes', without thinking, because I am married. He grabbed the form, glanced at it and shot me a withering glance. I surmised that I had inadvertently confirmed his poor opinion of the English, a decadent nation that not only allowed men to marry each other but had stolen the Islas Malvinas from their rightful owners, Argentina. But I may have been over-interpreting, beginning to hallucinate with fatigue. I had now been arguing at the front desk for over an hour. Then he suddenly announced that two single rooms had become available and threw the keys at me.

With a mixture of relief and anger we got up to the rooms we knew we should have been in all along without this irritation. In the slow, small lift I boasted to my brother-in-law that this was the only way to survive in Argentina – stand your ground and be as obstinate as they were. He was impressed. 'Bloody Argentines,' we said. Shower first and then we will go out to eat, we agreed. Didn't Argentina have the best steaks in the world? I got in the shower and savoured it, covering

140

myself in shower gel. I had hardly done it when the phone rang. I thought it might be my brother-in-law having trouble with his room. I got out, still covered in gel and bubbles, and padded across to the phone by the bed.

'Meester Weendsor?' said a female voice. 'Yes?' 'This is Juanita from agency you booked through.' 'Hello, Juanita, I am glad you phoned. We have had a terrible time getting…' She interrupted with emphasis, 'Meeester Weendsor, you are in wrong hotel.' Juanita claimed that we had indeed been booked into the Hotel Lafayette but they had changed it ten days ago as the agency had fallen out with the Lafayette. They had sent us a new voucher, she said. 'You must please to move to proper hotel.' I protested, but she would not have it. I rinsed myself off and phoned my brother-in-law's room telling him the unwelcome news. He took it well, and we dressed, repacked and left, passing the desk with Señor Miserable still on duty. He looked less suicidal, even a bit jubilant.

He had spoken to the agency and to Juanita, and said we should admit that he was right, we didn't have a booking. I ignored his triumphalism and as the taxi arrived I asked for my Ministry of Foreign Affairs form back. I didn't tell him why but I realised that it appeared from my declaration that my brother-in-law and I were married. 'No, señor, impossible, your declaration has already been sent over to the ministry.' So my brother-in-law and I are married, but only in Argentina.

Antarctica: A Russian ship (2006)

My brother-in-law and I, now married, according to the documentation submitted to the Argentine Ministry of Foreign Affairs, headed down to Ushuaia to board the ship for Antarctica. There were lots of anti-British graffiti down there, such Las Malvinas Argentinos. Our ship, Akademik Ioffe, formerly a Russian oceanographic vessel, was waiting for us the next day. Fortunately, news had not reached Ushuaia that we were married, and we were given two single cabins with an interconnecting bathroom with a door to each cabin on either side.

We left Ushuaia in the evening and started out through the Beagle Channel. A place forbidding and beautiful at the same time. Forbidding because of the silence, emptiness and desolation. It is at the end of the peopled world, beautiful in its grandeur and its pristine nature. We were seeing it in the same way that the first explorers had seen it; it has not changed in those five centuries. There is just one small community after Ushuaia, called Puerto Williams. It is on the Chilean side, the last buildings on the south American continent, facing out from black mountains into a dark sea, perched precariously and unsure at the continent's end. After that there is nothing except the empty lands of Chile on the right-hand side of the channel and Argentina on the other.

The politics of who the territory physically belongs to is made almost pointless by the fact that these are unpopulated, unused and vast spaces. On the Argentinean side the end of the Andes range extends right to the edge of the continent, steep, sharp pinnacles with snow daubed on the top valleys. The rock black in the mid-summer dusk. The Chilean side, where Tierra del Fuego finally slips into the sea, lower and forested, with rocky outcrops above the tree line. The whole channel a secret glide-way between pristine landmasses, enfolded in utter silence.

Then there appeared one small light ahead. The pilot's tug did not, as I would have imagined, follow us during the five-hour traverse of the narrowest part of the Beagle Channel. It lay waiting there in the midnight dim nestling, like a toy boat, in a small bay on the Chilean side. It seemed asleep even adrift but as we approached it came to life and gathered speed as it headed straight towards us. As it drew closer alongside, it did a sharp U-turn and sailed with us until the speed of the two vessels were identical. The pilot who had taken us through the channel for the last five hours descended from our vessel and elegantly stepped onto the tug which twirled again and returned to the cove it had come from, to await the next inbound vessel. I pictured the pilot and his two crewmen spending the night in this remote spot, waiting, as if in ambush, for the next customer.

I felt at ease in the haven of our boat, passing by one of the wildest and most uninhabited places on earth. Another passenger leant on the same rail; short, slim, with I thought Maori features. And so it was; she said she was a Maori but lived in Cairns, Australia. As dusk descended at about 11 p.m. she told me of the Maori ceremonies when someone died. It was irrelevant here, where no one lived or died. She was interested in living a natural life, even growing her own food. She said she would like to know how to propagate seeds, but didn't. Our conversation confused me as she said she worked in a 'club' in Cairns. She performed in the shows at the club. It was hard to square these two lifestyles in the one girl. But we chatted amiably, one not much understanding the other, in the silver light of the sub-Antarctic evening.

As we talked a small, barren island came into view, with a trawler, old, rusty and broken, wrecked on its rocks. That was the only thing we saw that would not have been there 500 years ago when Magellan passed by. Back then, this woman's Maori ancestors were still happily living their own lives, also undiscovered by the white man. I got to bed as the ship gently rocked its way south, still in the quiet protection of the Beagle Channel. But during the night we would leave that haven and start the traverse of the Drake Passage to Antarctica. I had heard of people being injured during this part of the journey, being thrown across the cabin and breaking a hip. I wondered if I would be awoken by huge waves but the passage to Antarctica was serene. One question kept me awake: what was a Maori lady, who worked in a nightclub in Cairns but was more interested in propagating seeds, doing in the Beagle Channel, heading for Antarctica?

France: Lot et Garonne (2014)

They seemed such a nice couple, Ruben and Lotte. Flemish Belgians, early retirement. He strong and stocky – he had been an ambulanceman in Bruges. She slim and boyish, quite muscular but anxious and restless. In Ghent she had been a saleswoman of pet foods. Whenever we saw her she said she was tired. They moved in as our neighbours 200 metres down the hill. The properties were beside a narrow country road through an avenue of old trees where a collaborator during the war was killed by La Résistance and buried; we were further up the hill, at the end of the road in the last house.

We had bought the house, in a small village in south-west France, a couple of years before they arrived. As I arrived to take possession of our new house (and my first-ever septic tank), there stood the previous owner busy unscrewing all the light fittings and bulbs, so by the time they handed over the keys and left us to our house it was night. The house sat on a ridge in a beautiful spot, but as the valley darkened and we sat there under the light of the one bulb he had thoughtfully left, we realised that our new property was full of dormice. They were not visible but we heard them; they were happily dwelling all over the house in the spaces behind the walls. Unfortunately, they kept the same hours as us, or a bit earlier in the morning and later at night.

They woke at around 5 a.m., squabbled as they left our house to find fruit and nuts, then came back just when we were going to bed. The squabbling got worse when they got back – maybe fighting over who got the day's fruit-and-nut haul. As I lay there on the first night, the

143

dormouse dispute continued just behind my head. The Romans thought them a gastronomic delicacy but I didn't want to try them sautéed or any other way, and Sally didn't want me to hurt them. But I wanted them out, so finally, by stopping up all the gaps in the cellar and the walls, they cleared off, maybe to the house next door then still empty.

When I saw that there were new people just moved in next door I called in to say bonjour. I floundered on in French until they intervened and asked if I spoke English. Ruben was extremely helpful, clever and practical. His wife Lotte perhaps a little odd but kind. It was a new adventure for them, they said they always dreamt of retiring early to a warmer climate like south-west France, doing up a house, installing a pool, keeping chickens, growing vegetables and flowers and getting away, so they said, from the Turkish immigrants in Belgium. They reinforced this with a curious example: they said that Muslim traffic wardens never gave parking tickets to other Muslims, only to the native Belgians.

We were not at our house in France often but, when we were, we got on well with them, and often invited each other to dinner. Ruben said he watched Fawlty Towers every single night in bed, and knew the scripts off by heart. He was marvellously practical; one day our roof leaked badly in a heavy storm and he brought over a ladder from next door and fixed it. When I showed him around our house I mentioned that Sally didn't like the varnished ceiling in our bedroom, she wanted it white. Next time we got to France he had done it. They both smoked heavily. She coughed a lot.

One day he came over to tell us that she had lung cancer and a surgeon would shortly operate at the hospital in Cahors to remove the part of her lung with the tumour. She had seen the surgeon several times before the operation. After the operation she stayed in hospital for a couple of weeks. When she came out she was weak, of course, but dreamy and preoccupied. She came to have tea one day and revealed that she had fallen very much in love, more in love than she had ever been in her whole life. More in love than she could ever have imagined. 'With whom?' we inquired. 'With my surgeon,' she said. Sally told her she had heard of this sort of thing happening but nothing ever came of it, he was a married man of high standing in Cahors. She should keep it as a fantasy and not even tell her husband or anyone else.

But she did tell him. He became very jealous, even though he must have known it to be fantasy. One day he came over in a hurry, and asked to borrow our car. 'Ruben, it's a hire car and you are not insured for it, but I will take you wherever you want to go'. He said he wanted to tail his wife, who had just left the house. He was sure Lotte had set off to see the surgeon in Cahors. But she would recognise his car. I declined to tail her, saying that it was a fantasy and to let her get it out of her system. But he was convinced that it was no fantasy, it was real; he said he had seen correspondence between them. He sped off in his own car and chased after her anyway.

He caught her up, but in Cahors he lost her and realised he didn't have the address of the surgeon's consulting rooms where Ruben was convinced there was a tryst. He stopped the car, phoned a friend and asked him to look up the surgeon's address and phone back urgently so that he could swiftly get there. No call came. After half an hour he called back his friend. 'Why didn't you call me back?' 'I did.' 'No, you didn't.' 'Yes, I definitely did, but it was engaged and I left a message.' 'Which number did you call?' asked Ruben. Months before, Ruben had given his phone to his wife and bought a new one for himself – but he hadn't told his friend. So his friend had inadvertently called Lotte's number and left the message for Ruben on her voicemail as to where she might be headed.

The trail went cold. Ruben continued to tail her but she announced that she had never loved him and she was even more madly in love with the surgeon. Ruben, deeply hurt, fell into the arms of a Flemish lady, recently divorced and living nearby. Lotte, gradually realising that her affair with the surgeon was unlikely ever to be consummated, decided to attack her rival to win back her husband. Meanwhile, he asked me if he could get away from the village and come to Edinburgh for a holiday. I agreed, but I did not know whom he would bring from the love triangle. It was the new lady, Pamela. They came, and Lotte found out about the trip.

Without being aware of it Sally and I were now in the crosshairs and had become a target. One evening later on, staying in our house with my children and grandchildren, ten of us in total, and we drove to the local village to the Marche Nocturne, the village dinner. This is a tradition in the area. There are lots of trestle tables laid out in the square beside the church. Local farmers, wine growers, cheese makers, bakers and so on set up stalls around the outside of the square, as do stallholders selling moules and frites, paella, roast chicken and the like. There is a band for dancing and a merry-go-round for the kids. It's a taste of rural France at its most convivial. The warm evening and bustling crowds made it fun for the grandchildren who zipped around the stalls and the tables while the teenage boys searched for French girls.

145

I had not expected it, but Ruben turned up at our table, and half an hour later so did Pamela. While we were there Ruben's phone pinged: a text message from Lotte. He read it and turned urgently to me. 'Lotte says your house has been burgled.' I rushed home with my daughters, thinking it might have been a 'call for attention' hoax, as she must have guessed that Ruben, Pamela and all of us were there together. It was not. The house had been trashed, the door smashed to gain access, windows shattered, mirrors too. The floors upstairs and down were covered in glass, the grandchildren's beds too. The TV, laptop and computer were destroyed, crockery broken, wardrobes emptied and items pulled onto the floor, but nothing stolen.

The gendarmes came; it was a crime of vengeance, they said. It was rare, but might happen when an already disturbed woman or man wanted to get at their husband or wife through his or her friends, to destroy their other relationships. Ruben came and saw the damage, but refused to believe it could have been his wife and became angry with me for suggesting it. He violently threw his phone against the wall and it shattered and lay there, adding marginally to the debris. But he didn't think that for long. He rushed next door to confront his wife. She was drunk and now starting to smash up their house.

He had just finished creating a new gîte attached to his house and the first visitors had just arrived. The holidaymakers, looking forward to their first dinner outdoors in the tranquillity of the French countryside, were treated to a night of drama, not exactly a five-star Trip Advisor experience. In full view and earshot of the guests, Lotte paused from her orgy of destruction, picked up the car keys and jabbed Ruben in the face with them. He called the police. Then she grabbed his wallet and passport and ran screaming to the car. She took off at high speed, bounced off the front fence, sped down the narrow lane between the avenue of trees at a rate to awaken even the dead collaborator, and veered into a ditch at the first bend. The car lay there, its engine still roaring.

The police, now returning for their second call of the night, found her there. They dragged her out of the wreck and took her back up the avenue of trees to home. The visitors, now getting ready for bed in France profonde, were treated to Scene Two of the drama as the police dragged in the drunk and bloodied hostess.

Scene Three occurred in the morning when an ambulance crew arrived to take Lotte to the mental hospital. She resisted strongly. Even the village mayor came up to help and Lotte gave the tourists a rousing display as she fought the crew, her husband and the mayor. The medics took her to a mental hospital in Cahors, the town of her adored surgeon.

Are we humans the only species that suffer from mental illness? Other mammals can live in fear of predators, have aggressive neighbours or struggle to find food, but this is a natural condition for them. Such fear and insecurity is normal for wild animals and it does not trigger mental illnesses. Animals appear to suffer mentally when enclosed in an unnatural state in zoos, as can be seen from their repetitive behaviour. The widespread nature of mental disorders in humans, even when we do not have to fight for food or territory, seems to be the price we pay for our intelligence. The same genes that made us smart also predisposed us to mental illness. Animals probably do not get too upset about adultery in their mate, though maybe penguins do?

Did the dream of Ruben and Lotte to live a new life turn ashen and broken because they too found themselves in an unnatural state, alone in the depths of a foreign country? I don't know, but I had to sweep up the ragged glass shards of their fantasies.

Ireland: Radisson room-share (2014)

My booking was at the Radisson Hotel, Dublin. I walked through the front door to the reception desk where a uniformed young lady with a nametag reading 'Siobhan' looked up from her screen and gave me one of those artificial reception desk smiles. But I liked that, it is always better than nothing. 'Good evening, sir. How can I help you?' (Actually, in Ireland they say 'sorr'.) 'I'd like to check in, please. My name is Windsor, Malcolm Windsor.' 'Sorr, you are most welcome to the Radisson Hotel, I will just bring up your booking.' (I think that means they will look at it, not regurgitate it.)

'Ah, yes, I see it, sorr and I see you are here for two nights and are sharing with Stephen Grobel.' I shook my head vigorously. 'No, I have never heard of Stephen Grobel and I am certainly not sharing a bedroom with him.' She seemed to disbelieve me, and typed vigorously into her computer making 'tch tch' noises. I peered at her nametag wondering how to pronounce her name. She stared at her screen. 'Our reservations system definitely shows you as staying for two nights and sharing a room with Steve Grobel.' Now he was 'Steve'; I didn't care for this suggestion of intimacy. 'Well, Siobhan,' I said, reading her nametag again and despite this still unsure how to pronounce her name I think it came out as 'Chiobevhan', (she wasn't impressed). 'Your

147

reservations system is wrong. I have never heard of Stephen Grobel and I have no intention whatsoever of sleeping with him.'

She gave a momentary smirk and a slight sigh as if she suspected that 'Steve' and I had fallen out. She typed even more vigorously, staring at the screen, and after what seemed like five minutes she looked up at me again. She resumed the receptionist's smile. 'Oh, don't worry, Mr Windsor, I have sorted it, here is your key, you're in room 333.' She looked over my shoulder at the guests queuing behind me. I didn't move. 'Thank you, Siobhan, but let's be clear, I am not sleeping with Stephen Grobel. Are you sure you have sorted that out? I must insist my room is not shared with Mr Grobel.' She looked pained, with a hint of impatience. 'No, sorr, definitely not shared with Mr Grobel.'

The other guests waiting to check in looked quite interested in this dialogue but I turned past them with relief and headed for the lift. I got to the third floor and found my way to room 333. My plastic key smoothly opened the door and... Guess who was in my bed? He was startled, of course. As was I. 'You must be Stephen Grobel,' I said. He was quite young, lively looking but very worried by this intrusion. 'How do you know that?' 'I just knew it would be you,' I said.

In Conclusion

Though some are worried that we will evolve into semi-robots, humans are still delightfully silly, odd, amusing, strange and crazy. We do adore fun and silliness. But there is a limit, it's not funny at all being crazy if it is a mental illness.

We remember only certain things that happen to us. We store these special memories in our brains which are almost certainly the most complex objects in the whole of the solar system. Yet a human brain weighs only about two or three pounds, it is 75% water and the rest is 60% fat; it is surprisingly the fattiest organ in the body.

We love the memories, at least most of them, that we have stored in this fatty grey mass. The brain has a huge capacity and as we get older, we accumulate increasingly large amounts of these memories and it gives us a comforting pleasure to find them in that mass of folded cells and pull them back out, recall them.

Especially when we have been in a long relationship and have many shared experiences, what can be nicer than remembering them together? When my mother died, my father said this was one of the worst things to bear, there was no one now who shared and understood his memories.

148

When we remember something because of a mad, eccentric, idiotic, frightening, funny or embarrassing element it is almost always linked to an encounter with another human. I doubt that robots will be as funny though they might turn out to be as frightening.

Maybe one day we will be able to download our memories in their entirety to a stick, or upload our memories to the Cloud – which sounds much nicer, more heavenly. In the meantime, when we die our memories die too and, like a broken hard drive, the data cannot be recovered. Sometimes in dementia our memories go even before we die. We all fear that almost more than anything else.

Dear reader, you have your own unique precious memories. Some you can share with others who experienced them with you and some are yours alone but the greater pleasure is in sharing them.

They make you who you are. They are you.